The Complete Security Guide for Executives

Other Books by Neil C. Livingstone

The War against Terrorism (1982)

Fighting Back:
Winning the War against Terrorism
with Terrell E. Arnold (1985)

America the Vulnerable:
The Threat of Chemical/Biological Warfare
with Joseph D. Douglass, Jr. (1987)

Beyond the Iran/Contra Crisis:
The Shape of U.S. Anti-Terrorism Policy
in the Post-Reagan Era
with Terrell E. Arnold (1988)

All titles available from Lexington Books

The Complete Security Guide for Executives

by
NEIL C. LIVINGSTONE

with
STEVE RYAN
DON FEENEY
DAVE CHATELLIER

and
Corporate Training Unlimited

Lexington Books

D.C. Heath and Company • Lexington, Massachusetts • Toronto

This book is published as part of the Lexington Books
Issues in Low-Intensity Conflict series,
Neil C. Livingstone, consulting editor.

Library of Congress Cataloging-in-Publication Data

Livingstone, Neil C.
The complete security guide for executives.

(Lexington Books issues in low-intensity conflict series)
Includes index.
1. Executives—Protection—United States—Handbooks, manuals, etc.
2. Security systems—United States—Handbooks, manuals, etc.
3. Business enterprises—United States—Security measures—
Handbooks, manuals, etc.
I. Title. II. Series.
HV8290.L58 1989 362.8'8 88-32650
ISBN 0-669-16777-0 (alk. paper)

Published simultaneously in Canada
Printed in the United States of America
International Standard Book Number: 0-669-16777-0
Library of Congress Catalog Card Number: 88-32650

The paper used in this publication meets the minimum requirements of American National Standard for Information Sciences—Permanence of Paper for Printed Library Materials, ANSI Z39.48-1984.

Year and number of printing:

89 90 91 92 8 7 6 5 4 3 2 1

This book is dedicated to my mother,
Jeanne C. Livingstone

Issues in Low-Intensity Conflict Series

Neil C. Livingstone, consulting editor

Beyond the Iran-Contra Crisis
The Shape of U.S. Anti-Terrorism Policy in the Post-Reagan Era
Neil C. Livingstone and Terrell E. Arnold, editors

The Complete Security Guide for Executives
Neil C. Livingstone

The Handbook for Effective Emergency and Crisis Management
Mayer Nudell and Norman Antokol

Low-Intensity Conflict
The Pattern of Warfare in the Modern World
Loren B. Thompson, editor

The Road to Kalamata
A Congo Mercenary's Personal Memoir
Mike Hoare

The Safe Travel Book
A Guide for the International Traveler
Peter Savage

Special Operations and National Purpose
Ross S. Kelly

Urgent Fury
The Battle for Grenada
Major Mark Adkin

Contents

Acknowledgments

I want to thank Steve Ryan, who provided outstanding research assistance to this project. In addition, Don Feeney, Dave Chatellier, and Robert W. Senseney, Jr., all of Corporate Training Unlimited, carefully scrutinized the manuscript for accuracy and gave me the benefit of their many years of operational experience regarding security matters. I am also grateful to Jaime Welch-Donahue, my superlative editor at Lexington Books for the past five years, and to Bob Bovenschulte and Steve Dragin, Lexington Books executives who took advantage of me in a moment of weakness and thereby made this book possible.

The Complete Security Guide for Executives

Only those means of security are good, are certain, are lasting, that depend on yourself and your own vigor.

—Niccolò Machiavelli

Introduction

WE live in a violent world. According to the Justice Department, theft or violent crime struck one in four households in the United States during 1987. You, your immediate family, or someone you know is likely to be touched by violent crime during your lifetime. And if crime is soaring in the United States, crime rates are even higher in many foreign countries.

Equally alarming is the growth of global terrorism. You may become a victim of terrorism not because of anything you've ever done, but simply because you're in the wrong place at the wrong time, because you work for an American company, or because of your religion or nationality. If you want to know what can be done to minimize your risk and to protect your family, your company, and your livelihood, this book is for you.

This book is designed for the busy business executive who does not have time to become an expert on security or to read lengthy accounts of terrorist incidents. You do not need to know who the leaders of a particular terrorist group are or their various ideologies. It's enough to know that they exist. I presume that you already know enough about crime and terrorism to regard them as serious threats.

Accordingly, I have developed this bare-bones reference guide to better security, written in layman's language. This book does not make recommendations that are unrealistic or just don't fit your lifestyle. Sure, you will be safer if you give up your company perks, dress like a bum, and don't travel, but you are not about to do so. Therefore, *The Complete Security*

Guide for Executives endeavors to lay out a security awareness program that is consistent with both your position and the responsibilities that go with the job.

I have assembled the book with the assistance of many advisers from government agencies, the private security industry, and businessmen who have expressed their dissatisfaction with other manuals on the market and offered suggestions for improving them. Several of those assisting in the compilation of this manual are former members of the elite U.S. Delta Force and have provided protection to U.S. ambassadors in some of the more difficult and dangerous spots in the world, including Beirut.

I also hope that you will find this book useful from a management point of view. Good personal and corporate security is not something that can be totally delegated to others. In the final analysis, it is your responsibility. This book is designed to make you, the corporate executive, more conversant with the elements of good security, as well as a better consumer of security products and services.

1

Personal Protection

THE latest rage for corporate executives who have grown bored with tennis camps and Club Med vacations is to attend one of the specialized schools offering counterterrorism instruction and training in self-defense methods. If running the Colorado River in a rubber raft just doesn't produce the high it used to, there are schools that purport to teach high-stress defensive combat shooting, civilian self-defense, elements of survival, shotgun techniques, and even something called warrior indoctrination. For $1,200 a week, one school offers students instruction in the martial arts, electronic countermeasures, sniping, use of combat pistols, situation awareness, use of unconventional weapons (hatchets, ballpoint pens, files, and screwdrivers), and convoy procedures.

While it may make someone's blood run a little faster to stand on a remote mountaintop in "cammies" and jump boots and watch a black-bereted instructor demonstrate an assault rifle, such training is unlikely to save that person's life if the crunch ever comes. Such skills generally take years to perfect. For the average corporate executive, a three-day course in special weapons instruction, close combat skills, and counterterrorist driving techniques is not of much practical value other than increasing his awareness of what constitutes good security.

Indeed, the security field is one place where a little knowledge can be dangerous. Too often executives and so-called security specialists with only limited training become overconfident and take unnecessary and often dangerous risks.

By contrast, good personal security depends chiefly on how you choose to live your life. It involves anticipating problems before they happen and reducing your vulnerabilities. In the final analysis, your goal should be to outthink terrorists and criminals, not try to outshoot them. If you live a prudent life, avoid routines, and take to heart the suggestions in this book, you will significantly reduce your chances of becoming a victim of violence.

Taking Some General Precautions

Be alert. The key to good personal security is constant vigilance. Vigilance means keeping your mind focused on danger signals and not on personal matters, business, or Sunday's football game. The terrorist or criminal is waiting for you to become distracted and to let down your guard. It is at that moment that he will strike. Remember, you can be ambushed in your own neighborhood.

Watch for muggers. Walk purposely and authoritatively after nightfall or in dangerous neighborhoods. Know who is behind you. A heavy cane or umbrella may discourage a common street mugger since he knows you can use either as a weapon.

Do not flash your cash. Watch at cashier lines for people who take an interest in the contents of your wallet or the wallets of others. Keep some loose bills in your pocket to hand over to a mugger.

In the event you are mugged, do not resist unless the mugger clearly means to harm you. Hand over your wallet and anything else the mugger wants. Your life is not worth your watch and the contents of your wallet.

Don't wear jewelry. It's a good idea not to wear jewelry on the street while traveling abroad. It is even dangerous to do so in some big cities in the United States. Gangs of roving youths in New York and Washington, D.C., grab gold chains from the necks of women pedestrians. In places such as Colombia, punks even rip gold earrings from women's pierced ears. Men also should avoid flashy jewelry, as it may simply invite a mugging.

Deter pickpockets. Distribute your money over several pockets to deter pickpockets. Carry your wallet in a pocket where you can feel someone tampering with it. In this connection, a shirt pocket is better than a hip pocket for detecting prying fingers. Men might consider purchasing a money belt or ankle wallet. Women should consider purchasing slips and other lingerie items with hidden pockets.

Remember that many pickpockets are women and children. Beware of children swarming around you. Gypsy children in Europe work in bands. Usually one child tries to distract you while another reaches into your purse or coat pocket. Street waifs in Latin America may seem adorable, but many earn their living as pickpockets. Similarly, a come-on by a streetwalker may actually be an attempt to pick your pocket. If someone bumps into you on the street, discreetly check to make sure your wallet is still there, but don't reveal the location of your valuables by patting yourself in an obvious fashion.

Do not chase a pickpocket, as he or she may turn on you with a knife or other weapon.

Avoid the back of the bus. If you are traveling by bus in a foreign country, never sit in the rear. First, you cannot communicate with the driver if you lose your bearings and have to ask where to get off. Second, you can be accosted in the rear of a crowded bus without the driver being aware of it.

Be alert on subways. When standing on a platform waiting for a subway, watch for people who seem inattentive to an approaching train. A real commuter will probably be looking up the track toward the approaching train, not scanning the other passengers. People who seem to be scouting around may be pickpockets, purse snatchers, or muggers.

Beware of taxis. Do not take the first taxi that zips up when you walk out of your hotel. The driver may have been waiting for you. A number of Americans have been kidnapped overseas in this fashion. If the taxis are lined up and you are required to take the one at the head of the line, you might want to consider stepping back and letting someone else go ahead of you until you see a taxi you feel comfortable with.

Don't be afraid to turn down a ride in a cab that appears unsafe or if the driver is acting strangely. If there is no meter in the cab, negotiate a price to your destination before you leave, not after you arrive. If you don't speak the language, have the hotel doorman negotiate the price with the driver.

Be mindful of briefcases and purses. When traveling abroad, hold on tight to bags, briefcases, and purses. Don't leave them unattended, even next to you, on the back seat of a taxi when traveling through a crowded urban area. In many Latin American countries, a street criminal might reach through the window, grab your bag, and take off on foot.

If you are a woman, always carry a purse with a strap and keep the purse close to your body, preferably underneath your arm. Never leave a purse unattended on a table or on the floor of a rest room stall. Someone might reach underneath from the next stall and grab it.

Never walk with your purse or bag open. Terrorists and drug smugglers have been known to drop items in open bags and then retrieve them once you have cleared customs or crossed a checkpoint.

Watch out for drunks and punks. If you are accosted by a drunk, try to ignore him. If that is impossible, distract him and move away. Remember, he may not really be drunk but instead might be a mugger or pickpocket.

When confronted by punks, try to ignore them. Concentrate on your newspaper or stare straight ahead. Do not make eye contact and pretend not to hear their taunts or cracks about you. A bruised ego is better than a battered head, so just ignore them and hope they move on to other prey. Whatever you do, don't show fear. Someone who shows fear is inviting trouble.

Mobs are always dangerous. Rampaging mobs are usually a by-product of political tension. Don't succumb to curiosity; civil disturbances are not a spectator sport. Stay away from political marches or sections of the city where rioting is likely to break out.

Riots are chaotic situations, and you run the risk of injury from both the police and the rioters. In some countries, if you are singled out as an American or European, the mob may vent its rage on you. By the same token, police may use rubber bullets and tear gas on rioters. You could be beaten with a baton and even arrested simply for being in the wrong place during a civil disturbance.

In some countries, riots occur in conjunction with sporting events. In Great Britain, if you read in the newspaper that Manchester United is to take the field against Standard Liege, watch out. If you want to avoid trouble, stay away from the stadium. If you suddenly find yourself surrounded by hooligans sporting a team logo and reeking of alcohol, join them in their chants. Doing as the Romans do is better than becoming their next human sacrifice.

Don't advertise your nationality. When traveling abroad, blend in with the native population. Don't dress like the typical American tourist. Leave T-shirts with slogans in English at home. Don't wear stars-and-stripes running shorts or other similar garb. You may be targeted for terrorist attack simply because you are American. A young American serviceman, for example, was murdered in West Germany for his identity card, which was later used by terrorists to gain access to an American military base.

The only time to break this rule is in a country such as Afghanistan, where Americans are the good guys and the Soviets are the bad guys. In the past, tall white males generally were presumed to be Russian advisers, so anyone who fit that description was fair game. U.S. reporters and television crews took to wearing small American flag patches on their shoulders so that no one would mistake them for Russians.

Stay away from tourist haunts. If you are fearful of terrorism while traveling abroad, avoid cafés, nightclubs, and other tourist spots that might be targeted by terrorists because of the high concentration of Americans usually found on the premises.

Use well-traveled streets. This will increase your safety. A busy street means that a criminal or terrorist has more to worry about in terms of being identified by passersby or by someone coming to your assistance. A busy street presents other logistical problems for terrorists as well.

Travel in pairs. Generally speaking, there is safety in numbers. This may not hold true when you are confronted by a determined terrorist gang armed with automatic weapons, but it does have a chilling effect on street criminals. They would much rather target a lone individual, especially a woman or an older person. In many foreign countries, women are much safer in the company of at least one other person, preferably a man. Walking with a man also will reduce the risk that a woman will be subjected to sexually explicit insults.

Carry a medical identification card. Information on the card should include allergic reactions to any medication, susceptibility to insect stings, recent vaccinations, name and telephone numbers (both office and home) of your physician, and whether you wear contact lenses.

Keep a low profile. If you are a prominent person, don't announce your visit in advance. Articles and photos in the newspaper only increase your risk, since they may alert criminals and terrorists to your presence. Never allow material regarding your itinerary, flight plans, or hotel to be published. You may even want to make your reservations under an alias or in the name of a traveling companion.

Detecting Surveillance

Spotting a "tail." Terrorist attacks are usually preceded by a period of surveillance. Watch for it and learn how to recognize that you are under surveillance. If you "make" your tail, you are likely to discourage the terrorists from carrying out their operation. At the very least, you will be on your guard.

Bad guys seldom wear trench coats. Do not expect to see a Sam Spade type in a trench coat. Your tail is likely to be someone you least expect, such as a woman or an elderly man. The Irish Republican Army (IRA) even uses children to carry out surveillance work. What you are looking for is one or more individuals who pop up more than once on your route.

Alternating tails. Do not expect to see the same tail constantly. Surveillance is often carried out by teams, with one person directly behind you and others farther back to relieve the "close-in" tail. Other tails may be traveling parallel to you on the other side of the street or on parallel streets. They may use radios if in vehicles or walkie-talkies if on foot.

Unalterable items or characteristics. The tail may have a bagful of wigs, glasses, snap-on ties, and reversible jackets. Try to concentrate on details such as height and facial characteristics. Look for things that cannot be changed quickly, such as trousers or shoes, and personal items such as rings and other jewelry that tend to be overlooked even by professionals in surveillance.

Driving tricks. A surveillance vehicle may pass you and allow you to overtake it. This occurs naturally in heavy traffic, and the tail often will use it to his advantage.

Headlight tricks. Some surveillance teams rig their headlights to look alternately like a sedan and a motorcycle. One headlight will be rigged with a switch that permits it to be turned off and on at will. When it is turned off, you will see a single headlight in your rearview mirror. This is designed to make you believe that the suspicious sedan you saw earlier is gone.

Taillight tricks. Inspect your taillights. If you find a small hole in one of them, it may be that you are under surveillance. An old surveillance trick that allows the tail to stay well back of his subject at night, even on a crowded road, is to punch a small hole in one of the taillights. The taillight will have a bright white spot instead of being totally red or amber. A clever professional also may put a high-intensity bulb in one of your taillights, leaving the low-intensity bulb in the other. Similarly, he may simply remove one of your taillight bulbs.

Tracking devices. Do not underestimate the surveillance team's sophistication. A clever professional may place a strip of light-reflecting tape on your bumper or even attach one of a variety of miniature tracking or homing devices to your car to assist in tailing you. Be on the lookout for such things during your daily bomb check (see chapter 4).

Countering Surveillance

Try speeding up, then slowing down. An inexperienced tail will break into a trot to catch up or be confused as to how he can mask his own reduction in speed. This may work both on foot and in your car.

Step to the side or pull over. Take note of the characteristics of the people and vehicles behind you. If you are driving, try to get the license plate numbers of cars that are following you. Do this several times to see who, if anyone, keeps on accidentally (but on purpose) turning up behind you. Remember that tails may be operating in teams, with others traveling on parallel streets or keeping in touch by radio. The same car or person may not turn up consistently but will eventually reappear. Just because you make one tail, does not mean you have made them all.

Turn in your tracks. If you do this, you may "roll up" several tails. Walk or drive by them, taking note of distinguishing characteristics and other important details. At this point, many tails will realize that they have been compromised and may go on to other targets, concluding that you are too alert. Alternatively, a new team might take over, so keep up your guard.

Stop to look in a store window. If you are on foot, this will provide you with an opportunity to see who is tailing you in the reflection.

Walk into a building and stop abruptly. Your tail may come blundering in, only to be confronted by you face-to-face.

Drop something to see if someone picks it up.

Get on subways or buses at the last minute. You have probably seen this trick in the movies.

If you are not alone, have another member of your group stop or drop back to monitor who passes by.

Know who your neighbors are. Always know who your neighbors are, both at home and in your place of business.

Make a point of dropping in on new neighbors to check them out. They may actually be a surveillance team.

Monitor citizens band and other radio frequencies. If you have personal or corporate security, they should periodically monitor or scan citizens band (CB) and other radio frequencies in the area to determine if anyone is following you.

Train your household staff. Your household staff should watch for strange vehicles or persons lingering around your house. Beware of delivery men, messengers, or "lost" persons who approach your house to ask for directions or use the telephone. Your office staff also should be on the alert for strange individuals who might be casing the area.

Eluding a Tail

If you are a woman, go directly to a police officer and point out the individual. Do this on your first suspicion. Police are used to handling complaints by women who are being harassed by weirdos, and they will usually give a woman the benefit of the doubt. While a man may be regarded as a crank, a woman will usually get some action. At the very least, the police officer will generally approach the tail and ask what he is doing. The tail will probably have a ready explanation, but the cop may hold him up long enough for you to give him the slip.

If you are a woman and your tail is a man, try losing him in a woman's shop or bathroom. The tail's bagful of wigs and costumes, no matter how elaborate, will probably be inadequate for him to continue the chase. Consider lingering in the lingerie department of a department store, where the tail should be easy to make.

Change your appearance. Duck into a store and buy a hat or jacket that will alter your appearance. You may be able to slip out the door and into the crush of pedestrians without the tail realizing what you have done.

Take an elevator. If you are in a large city, enter a tall building and take a busy elevator. Get off at any floor and take the first elevator back down to the lobby. Again, if you can remove your coat, slip on dark glasses, or change your appearance in some way, you may be able to elude the tail's attention, even if he is still waiting in the lobby.

Should you lose your tail, expect him to try to relocate you. He may wait for you at your home or office or attempt to call you, so expect to get one of those "Sorry, wrong number" calls.

Practice makes perfect. An experienced tail will be difficult to elude without substantial practice on your part. A number of security firms offer one- or two-day courses in detecting and eluding surveillance. You might want to consider taking a course of this kind.

Defending Yourself in Unarmed Combat

This manual cannot teach you the elements of hand-to-hand combat in a few easy lessons; only an experienced instructor working with you for many months can do that. It takes even longer to become a martial arts expert, as well as above-average reflexes and excellent conditioning. This section gives you a few basic moves and techniques that can save your life.

Always defend yourself as though fighting for your life. This is not the movies: Fight dirty and never give your opponent a break. Be savage. Don't rely on one good punch; throw as many blows as possible at your opponent, as swiftly as possible. Once your opponent is down, continue striking him until you are certain that he can't get up; don't give him a chance to recover.

In general, keep your opponent at a distance. Use your feet or throw things at him to keep him from closing and grappling with you. This is particularly valuable advice for women, since most women are not as strong as their male attackers.

Aim a blow at the side of the attacker's neck. Major arteries are located there. A strong blow could incapacitate your assailant.

Jab straight out at the assailant's Adam's apple or grab the front of his throat. The blow might collapse his windpipe or sever the cartilage there.

Hit your assailant in the temple or behind the ear.

Hit, kick, or punch any area of the assailant's spinal cord or the back of his neck.

Kick the assailant under the arm, between the legs, or in the stomach.

Cup your hands and slap them over your assailant's ears. Football players often use this type of blow to stun their opponents. The concussion to the eardrums will cause dizziness and extreme pain.

If your assailant is on top of you, chomp down with your teeth on his ears, grab his nostrils, or jam a finger in his eyes.

If you are grabbed from behind, stamp on your assailant's feet, kick backward at his shins, or reach behind you and grab or smash his testicles. Your elbows also are very effective weapons. Swing them back against the assailant's rib cage or up into his throat.

Using Improvised Weapons

You can turn many ordinary items into effective, if not lethal, weapons.

Sharp objects. Any sharp object, such as a pen or pencil, can be used like a knife to jab an assailant. Aim for the eyes. Even a comb can be used to slash at an attacker.

Keys. Keys held in the palm of your hand, their points protruding between your fingers, can be used to slash an opponent.

Belts. A belt with a heavy buckle can be swung as a whip. A bicycle chain also can be used like a whip.

Aerosol sprays. Various aerosol sprays—oven cleaners, hair sprays, or deodorant sprays—can be used to blind an attacker. Spray paint is a very effective weapon that also marks your attacker. Bleach also can be thrown in the attacker's eyes. Remember to hold your breath or put your hand over your mouth and nostrils when using an aerosol spray against an attacker.

Canes, umbrellas, and nightsticks. Any truncheonlike object can be aimed at the inside of an adversary's wrists, his elbows, or his kneecaps.

Ordinary objects. Almost any item in a room can be adapted to self-defense. A drinking mug can be used to break an attacker's collarbone. A lamp can be wielded as a club. A light bulb, held by the base with a cloth or towel to protect your hand, will result in dozens of painful cuts if smashed into an adversary's face.

Blackjacks. Any heavy object—pocket change, a bar of soap, or a coffee mug—can be slipped into a sock or wrapped in an article of clothing and swung like a blackjack.

2

Traveling Abroad

"THE world is a country which nobody ever yet knew by description," wrote Lord Chesterfield to his son. "One must travel through it one's self to be acquainted with it." Lord Chesterfield's advice to his son underscores the central theme of this chapter: While traveling to other lands can, at times, be hazardous, the benefits far outweigh the risks. No American should hesitate to see and experience different countries and cultures. No corporation should, out of fear, reject the need to open markets and expand operations abroad.

Jet travel and instantaneous communication have linked parts of the world as never before. As a result, economic and political isolationism is no longer feasible for any but the most xenophobic and backward nations. Given this reality, American business must not only compete for world resources and markets, but it must compete more successfully than its rivals if the United States is to maintain its prosperity and security.

Thus, travel is an indispensable element of modern corporate life. While there certainly are risks associated with travel, especially to some parts of the globe, one must keep several facts in mind. First, it is still safer to travel almost anywhere by airplane than it is to drive on most U.S. highways. Second, you already live in one of the most violent and crime-ridden societies on earth. Although it may be little consolation, you have as much, if not more, chance of being the victim of crime or violence in many major U.S. cities than in most places abroad. It is, believe it or not, much safer to walk down a street in Belfast, Northern Ireland, which is plagued by endemic sectarian violence, than a street in Detroit, the murder capital of the United States.

Third, the ordinary American's chances of being killed or injured in a terrorist attack or being taken hostage are relatively slim. Calculated from the actuarial tables, the average American's chances of being killed in a terrorist attack are less than the possibility of accidental death due to a fall, being struck by lightning, poisoning, fire, a motor vehicle crash, and virtually every other category of accidental death for which the U.S. Public Health Service keeps figures. If you are a diplomat, a member of the military, or a corporate executive in some parts of the world, however, your chances of being killed in a terrorist attack rise significantly, and you should adopt certain precautions to minimize your risk.

Preparing for a Trip

Know as much about each country you plan to visit as possible. Learn about the history, religion, geography, and government of every country on your itinerary. Have your staff provide you with a list of common phrases in the dominant language of each country. Important words and phrases include the following: "It's a pleasure to meet you," "Thank you," "Where is the bathroom?" "police," and "Help!"

Don't book your reservations with an unfamiliar travel agent. Make certain that your travel agent observes basic security precautions and keeps your travel plans confidential. You may want to consider booking your reservations under an alias. Never use your company name or your corporate, military, or diplomatic title in high-risk areas.

Obtain a passport. If you do not have one already, you can obtain a passport from the U.S. Passport Office or your local post office. You must provide proof of your U.S. citizenship. This proof can be a certified copy of your birth certificate, a previous passport, or, if you were not born in the United States, a naturalization certificate or statement from the clerk of the court attesting to your naturalization. You also must provide two identical front-view photos and fill out a passport application form. It takes approximately ten days to process your passport request.

Make certain that your passport is correct and that it has not expired before your return date. If you are traveling on official U.S. government business, you might want to carry your personal blue passport in addition to your diplomatic passport. In the event that your aircraft is hijacked, you can provide terrorists with your personal passport instead of your official passport. One Texas company will even sell you a phony passport, which is legal as long as you turn it over only to hijackers and don't try to use it for identification or to enter or exit a country.

Pay attention to what your passport may tell others about you. Consider getting a new one if you have an Israeli immigration control stamp in it or if your passport identifies you as either a businessman or government employee. Note: Israel has a system to avoid stamping its country's name in your passport.

Never lose sight of your passport. When traveling, always keep your passport on you. Don't let anyone except immigration officials or police officers have it. In some countries, you may have to leave it temporarily with the registration desk when you check in at a hotel. Never, however, leave it in your hotel room or luggage, where it can be stolen.

If your passport is lost or stolen, contact the nearest U.S. embassy or consulate. It helps if you have a photocopy of the front page of your passport, extra passport photos, and a copy of your birth certificate.

Obtain a visa. Many countries require visas before you enter or if you are planning an extended stay. To find out if a visa is required, contact the embassy or consulate of each country you are planning to visit or write for the booklet *Visa Requirements of Foreign Governments* (Passport Office Publication M-264), which is available from Passport Services, U.S. Department of State, Washington, DC 20524.

Some countries also require health records and certain inoculations. Be aware that many countries take weeks, even months, to process visa applications, so apply well in advance of your trip.

Evaluate the necessity of your trip. When considering travel to regions beset by terrorism or chronic political instability, ask yourself whether your trip is absolutely necessary. Can you accomplish your task by using the telephone or some other method?

Update your will. Don't read too much into this suggestion, but keeping your will current makes sense, especially before you travel. You also may want to give a power of attorney to a trusted member of your family, to be exercised if you meet with some misfortune. Establish a joint checking account for your spouse. Finally, leave behind a record of payments that need to be made (mortgage, car payment, and so on) during a protracted absence.

Check on travel advisories. Before traveling to a potentially dangerous region of the world, you may want to contact the State Department's Citizen Emergency Center (202–647–5225) for any warnings regarding your particular destination. Such information also is available by writing to Citizen Emergency Center, Office 4811, 2201 C Street NW, Washington, DC 20520.

Traveling by Plane

Flying coach. If you travel a great deal, flying first class may be the only thing that makes flying bearable, but you should know that flying coach is safer than flying first class. First class is in the front of the aircraft, either below (on a 747) or behind (on virtually all other aircraft) the cockpit. Terrorists generally turn the first-class section into their command area. Unless the terrorists move you into another part of the plane, you will be in close proximity to them if they open fire on the passengers. Moreover, should there be a rescue attempt, you run a greater risk of being caught in the cross fire.

In addition, first-class passengers are presumed by terrorists to be the wealthiest, most important people on board. They will probably focus more attention on first-class passengers than on those traveling in coach. It is far easier to blend into the crowd in the coach section of the cabin than in first class.

Don't dress to the nines. Curb your vanity. Expensive suits and jewelry draw attention to you. In particular, leave religious jewelry at home. You will be more comfortable in casual clothing, especially if you are hijacked.

Avoid aisle seats. Passengers located on the aisle are generally subjected to the most abuse. If a rescue operation takes place, most of the shooting will be directed down the aisles as the rescuers fight their way into the plane. If the shooting starts, you will be glad you tolerated the inconvenience of a window seat, as other people and seats will give you some protection.

In many respects, the safest seats are window seats adjoining an escape hatch (usually located over the wing). Be aware, however, that these are prime entry points for the assault team if an attempt to rescue the passengers is made. If you are handicapped, the airline will not permit you to sit in front of a hatch, fearing that you might block the exit in an emergency.

Try booking a flight on a large aircraft. Although air pirates are becoming far more sophisticated, the hijacking of a Boeing 747 requires far more manpower and effort than seizing a smaller jetliner. This is likely to discourage hijackings by lone skyjackers or small groups. A 747 is, however, far more difficult to rescue than other jetliners.

Choose your airline carefully. Some airlines are more likely to be targeted than others. While U.S. airlines, West Germany's Lufthansa, and Israel's El Al are known to have excellent security, this is attributable in large measure to the fact that they have all been targeted by terrorists in the past. In addition, India's national airline has been the target of Sikh attacks and Kuwait's national airline has been singled out by Shiite terrorists. The safest airlines tend to be those from places such as Sweden, Switzerland, Singapore, and Hong Kong, which are not members of major political blocs or embroiled in local conflicts. Although their service tends to be poor, national airlines from communist nations are targeted far less often than their free world counterparts. Also be aware that many Third World airlines, and a few airlines from industrialized states, have very poor safety records.

Find out where your flight originates. In addition, ask where it stops en route. If it puts down in a hot spot or a nation with poor airport security, the risk of explosives or terrorists being on board increases.

Try to minimize the number of stopovers. Flying the most direct route possible will minimize the risk of explosives or terrorists being on board and also decrease the amount of time you spend sitting in a vulnerable airport terminal.

Avoid countries with permissive attitudes toward terrorism. Airport security is the final line of defense, not the first line of defense, in preventing aviation-related terrorism. Good airport security cannot, by itself, redress the permissive policies toward terrorism embraced by some governments. Greece, for example, will remain a dangerous transit point so long as the government fails to take effective measures to combat terrorism.

Check your calendar. Terrorists often carry out attacks to commemorate key dates such as religious holidays, historical events, and the anniversary of terrorist attacks. Iran's independence is celebrated from January 16 to February 11. The Provisional IRA likes to commemorate Internment Day in August. The Palestine Liberation Organization (PLO) has Black September. Depending on your itinerary, you may want to take note of the following dates:

- January 1, Cuban revolution that brought Fidel Castro to power
- January 8, Palestinian memorial day
- January 15, birth of Gamal Abdel Nasser (Egypt)
- January 23, overthrow of dictator Marcos Perez Jimenez (Venezuela)
- January 30, Bloody Sunday (Northern Ireland)
- January 30, assassination of Mahatma Gandhi (India)
- February 1, return from exile of Ayatollah Khomeini (Iran)
- February 5, founding of National Liberation Army (Colombia)
- February 20, death of Cesar Augusto Sandino (Nicaragua)
- February 27, death of Armenian Secret Army for the Liberation of Armenia (ASALA) leader Yanikian (Turkey)
- March 13, death of M-19 leader Alvaro Fayad (Colombia)
- March 15, National Front for the Liberation of Angola (FNLA) day (Angola)
- March 17, St. Patrick's Day (Ireland)
- March 20, death of M-19 leader Carmenza (Colombia)
- March 21, International Solidarity Day for Palestinians
- March 23, Republic Day (Pakistan)

- March 24, beginning of British direct rule in Northern Ireland
- March 24, assassination of Bishop Romero (El Salvador)
- March 29, founding of New People's Army (NPA) (Philippines)
- March 31, overthrow of leftist president Goulart (Brazil)
- March 31, killing of three communist leaders (Chile)
- April (entire month), Month of Revenge, dedicated by Armenians to commemorate genocide by Turks
- April 1, Cyprus National Day Struggle for Independence
- April 1, founding of FPL (El Salvador)
- April 2, invasion of Falkland Islands (Argentina)
- April 4, founding of Syria's Baath party (Syria)
- April 4, execution of former president Zulfikar Ali Bhutto (Pakistan)
- April 8, founding of Iraq's Baath party (Iraq)
- April 9, 1981 bloodbath (Bolivia)
- April 9, 1973 Israeli raid on Beirut (Palestinian)
- April 13, founding of Sikh religion (India)
- April 15, U.S. air raid on Tripoli (Libya)
- April 15, birth of North Korean president Kim Il-Sung
- April 17, Syria's Independence Day
- April 17, Bay of Pigs invasion (Cuba)
- April 19, founding of M-19 terrorist group (Colombia)
- April 19, Day of Victory (Cuba)
- April 19, anniversary of Student Revolt (South Korea)
- April 24, National Day of Sorrow for Armenians (Turkey)
- May 3, Constitution Day (Japan)
- May 5, death of Bobby Sands (Northern Ireland)
- May 13, attack on Pope John Paul II
- May 18, founding of Shining Path (Peru)

- May 20, Cuban Independence Day
- May 22, Republic Day (Sri Lanka)
- May 30, Lod Airport massacre by Japanese Red Army (Israel)
- May 31, Republic Day (South Africa)
- June 5, Revolution Day/National Day of Mourning (Iran)
- June 5, Six-Day War (Israel)
- June 6, government attack on Sikh Golden Shrine (India)
- June 7, founding of National Revolutionary Movement (Bolivia)
- June 16, Soweto riots (South Africa)
- July 1, Communist Party Day (China)
- July 1, Canada Day/Dominion Day (Canada)
- July 1, death of Juan Peron (Argentina)
- July 4, Entebbe raid (Israel)
- July 4, U.S. Independence Day
- July 5, Venezuela's Independence Day
- July 5, overthrow of President Zulfikar Ali Bhutto (Pakistan)
- July 9, Argentine Independence Day
- July 18, National Uprising Day/Civil War (Spain)
- July 18, death of Benito Juarez (Mexico)
- July 19, Sandinista revolution (Nicaragua)
- July 21, Bloody Friday (Northern Ireland)
- July 28, Peru's Independence Day
- July 31, founding of the Basque ETA (Spain)
- July 31, kidnapping of U.S. Agency for International Development (AID) official Dan Mitrione by Tupamaros guerrillas (Uruguay)
- August 11, Internment Day (Northern Ireland)
- August 12, anniversary of British troops arriving in Northern Ireland (Northern Ireland)

- August 13, birth of Fidel Castro (Cuba)
- August 14, Independence Day/anniversary of President Mohammed Zia ul-Haq taking power (Pakistan)
- August 15, South Korean Independence Day
- August 15, India's Independence Day
- August 21, assassination of Benigno Aquino (Philippines)
- August 25, Uruguay's Independence Day
- September 1, anniversary of Muammar Qaddafi's revolution (Libya)
- September 5, attack at Munich Olympic Games (Palestinian)
- September 7, Brazil's Independence Day
- September 9, death of Mao Tse-tung (China)
- September 11, coup/death of President Salvador Allende (Chile)
- September 12, Revolution Day (Ethiopia)
- September 14, assassination of Christian president-elect Bechir Gemayel (Lebanon)
- September 15, El Salvador's Independence Day
- September 15, Honduras's Independence Day
- September 15, Nicaragua's Independence Day
- September 15, Guatemala's Independence Day
- September 16, Mexico's Independence Day
- September 18, Chile's Independence Day
- September 20, bombing of U.S. embassy in Beirut (Lebanon)
- September 22, anniversary of Iraq declaring war on Iran (Iraq/Iran)
- September 23, Saudi Arabia's National Day
- September 27, Basque Nationalist Party Day (Spain)
- September 28, death of Gamal Abdel Nasser (Egypt)

- October 1, Nigeria's Independence Day
- October 1, National Day (China)
- October 6, Yom Kippur War (Israel)
- October 7, Heroic Guerrilla Day/Death of Che Guevara (Cuba)
- October 8, birth of Juan Peron (Argentina)
- October 9, North Korean–sponsored bombing of South Korean cabinet delegation in Burma
- October 10, Kruger Day (South Africa)
- October 10, founding of FMLN (El Salvador)
- October 11, founding of MIR (Chile)
- October 18, death of Baader-Meinhof leaders (West Germany)
- October 23, bombing of U.S. Marine headquarters in Beirut (Lebanon)
- October 26, assassination of President Chung Ha Park (South Korea)
- October 31, assassination of Prime Minister Indira Gandhi (India)
- November 4, seizure of U.S. embassy in Tehran (Iran)
- November 6, M-19 attack on Palace of Justice (Colombia)
- November 15, Anglo-Irish Accord (Northern Ireland)
- November 25, unsuccessful left-wing coup in Portugal
- November 25, most sacred day for Sikh religion (India)
- November 27, birth of Benigno Aquino (Philippines)
- November 29, proclamation of state of Israel
- December 10, founding of Popular Front for the Liberation of Palestine (Palestinian)
- December 10, Popular Movement for the Liberation of Angola day (Angola)
- December 10, Constitution Day (Thailand)

- December 12, bombing of U.S. embassy and other targets in Kuwait by al-Dawa party (Iraq/Iran)
- December 17, Colombian Independence Day
- December 26, birth of Mao Tse-tung (China)
- December 27, Kenya's Independence Day
- December 31, founding of Philippine Communist party

Don't carry anything on you that identifies your religious or ethnic background. Try to carry identification that bears only your name and address. If someone demands an I.D. during a hijacking, offer them this.

Don't carry political literature. You never know who might take offense. Similarly, don't carry pornographic literature, especially in the Middle East. Leave business papers in your luggage, particularly those that might be sensitive or embarrassing. Remember, however, that your luggage may be searched (as it was during the hijacking of TWA flight 847 to Beirut in 1985).

Stationery bearing the letterhead of a multinational corporation or defense contractor might get you in trouble, even if the stationery is not your own. You may not be able to convince terrorists that such organizations are merely clients, and they might not even care about such distinctions.

Keep the purpose of your trip confidential. If you choose to do so, have an alibi ready and deliver it with confidence. Do not make your captors suspicious by fumbling around, breaking eye contact, and giving contradictory explanations. The best way to avoid this type of situation is to be prepared in advance.

File a trip plan with someone you trust. Make a point of checking in with him or her at frequent intervals. Brief the person on what to do if he or she does not hear from you.

Have a supply of necessary medications in your carry-on luggage. This makes especially good sense when you consider how often airlines lose luggage. Such a precaution could be a lifesaver if you have to endure a long siege or hijacking. Do not forget to carry a card with your blood type and necessary medical information. Also do not neglect the well-being of those accompanying you. Carry extra diapers and formula for young children and extra medication for the elderly in your party.

Don't drink excessively while flying. It will impair your ability to keep your wits and avoid trouble.

Checking In at the Terminal

Don't spend more time than is necessary in the airport, especially in unsecured areas. Terrorists have repeatedly targeted airport crowds, as was the case with the 1985 Rome and Vienna attacks where terrorists opened fire with automatic weapons and grenades.

Inquire about any last minute delays by telephone. When you get to the airport, check in quickly, go through security, and wait in a secured passenger area or immediately board the plane.

Consider using the lounges set aside for airline club members. While some are not located behind the security checkpoints, all are segregated from the general airport crowd and make less inviting targets. While there is usually an annual fee associated with membership, this writer knows of no airport attack that occurred in an area reserved for club members.

Always sit with your back to a wall. That way, you can see everything that is going on.

Avoid sitting near windows to reduce your vulnerability to flying glass (from bombs) and shots from outside.

Try to stand or sit near pillars or other building supports that will provide cover in a crisis. Be aware of your surroundings. While standing in line waiting to check in, imagine what you would do if terrorists suddenly burst into the airport. Where would you hide or take cover? Notice vending machines, sofas, and other things behind which you could duck if shooting broke out. As one former commando put it, "Keep in mind, if they don't see you, they won't shoot you."

When checking in as a group, minimize your exposure at the counter. Have one person check in for everyone while the rest of the group stays back from the throng.

Check your bags at the counter and not at curbside. Many airports no longer permit curbside checking anyway. Lock your luggage to prevent someone from slipping drugs or a bomb into one of your bags. Identify each piece with your name and address but never with the name of your company or government affiliation. If a stranger asks you to carry something aboard the plane, refuse and immediately notify someone from security.

Stay away from unattended bags. They could contain a bomb. Avoid trash bins, telephone booths, and other enclosures that could contain an explosive.

If anything looks suspicious, notify the authorities. Do not be bashful about reporting any passenger who behaves in a peculiar fashion or looks out of place. Most Americans are too polite, and thus too reluctant, to point the finger at someone. It is amazing how often other passengers have picked out terrorists and hijackers in their midst before an attack occurs but did not say anything for fear of offending the person if they were wrong.

Don't rubberneck. If there is a commotion or you see security people descending on an area, walk in the opposite direction (do not run, lest your retreat be regarded as suspicious).

Hit the ground the minute you hear shooting or an explosion. Pull your arms up over your head for even more protection. It may sound callous, but if you are caught in an open area during a terrorist attack, other people also may provide you with cover.

Don't let down your guard once the trip is over. Do not join the crowd at the baggage carousel. Your bags may take a while to get there, and those pressed around the carousel offer an inviting target.

Dealing with a Hijacking

Your chances of being hijacked are very slim, so don't spend too much time worrying about a potential hijacking. If you should find yourself on a hijacked plane, you can do certain things to increase your chances of surviving.

Some airlines carry armed guards or sky marshals. If such guards are on board, they may attempt to prevent the terrorists from taking over the plane. Stay alert and be prepared to drop to the floor or to scrunch down and cover up in the early moments of a hijacking. Come up only when you are sure the firing has stopped. Whatever you do, don't stand up and look around at the commotion. Invariably, a passenger who jumps up is killed or injured in the cross fire.

Don't give the hijackers any reason to mistake you for a sky marshal. The terrorists may be operating in teams, and not all of them may reveal themselves at the outset of the incident. They may be sitting among the passengers ready to kill anyone who looks like an undercover guard. Do not make any sudden movements, and do not reach into your jacket or luggage.

Explosion on the plane. If a bomb goes off, there may be a dramatic decompression in the plane's interior, with people and objects being sucked toward the hole. Keep your seat belt on to prevent becoming a casualty.

Follow the instructions of the flight crew. They are trained to deal with such contingencies. Don't initiate action on your own except in extreme circumstances. Think before you do anything. A calm, steady demeanor will reassure the other passengers.

Don't do anything to call attention to yourself. This is the most important rule for surviving a hijacking. Try not to make eye contact with any of the terrorists. Don't complain. Make youself inconspicuous. Maintain a neutral composure; don't show fear or anger if you can help it.

If you require medication or have some other severe medical problem, let your captors know about it. Otherwise, keep still. There is no reason why terrorists should give you special treatment, and your disturbance may single you out for abuse.

Don't ask questions. Not only will you call attention to yourself, but you may antagonize your captors. They will announce to you everything they are prepared to share.

Don't curry favor with the terrorists. They generally have little respect for those who grovel before them. Recognize your responsibility to the other passengers. Remember, there is a strong likelihood that you will survive, and the other hostages will remember any effort on your part to identify with the hijackers or seek their approval.

Be prepared for the worst. Your captors are likely to be violent and arbitrary. Don't try to reason with them. Never underestimate their depravity. If they are desperate enough to hijack an aircraft, they are capable of reacting unpredictably to the slightest provocation. They are likely to be very jittery; few hijackers have ever commandeered a plane before. It will take them a while to settle down. Don't do anything that will force them to react thoughtlessly out of fear or anger.

In addition, they will probably attempt to intimidate and humiliate you and the other passengers. Take their abuse without complaint. Should you antagonize them, they may single you out later for retribution.

Eat and drink as much as possible. Meals are likely to appear on an irregular basis. Don't be a prima donna; consume what you are served. You don't know how long you will be held hostage, so keep up your strength by eating when you have the opportunity to do so.

Expect to be uncomfortable. An aluminum cylinder parked on a concrete tarmac can get very hot in the summer and very cold in the winter. Moreover, you are likely to feel cramped and stiff. In the aftermath of a hijacking, most passengers remember the stench more than anything else. Initially, you and the other passengers may not be permitted to use the bathrooms, or you may be allowed to use them only infrequently. Passengers may be forced to relieve themselves in their seats. Later, when in use, the toilets are likely to overflow. Toilet paper will be in short supply. If it is any consolation, remember that the heat (or cold), stench, and cramped conditions are likely to be a problem for the terrorists as well and may contribute to a resolution of the crisis.

Take a mental picture of the situation inside the plane. In the event that you are released or escape, you may be able to provide valuable information to the authorities. They will want to know:

The number of hijackers and what they are wearing

Their race, sex, and other physical characteristics

Any clues you can provide about their nationality, identity, and language capabilities

Any routines the hijackers have established

The general location of the terrorists and the hostages

A description of the weapons carried by the terrorists and any explosives they have planted on board, as well as a report of any other preparations to repel a rescue attempt

Know how to get out of the plane in a hurry. Memorize where the exits are. Specifically memorize how many rows fore and aft of your seat the nearest exit is. If all hell breaks loose and the plane is full of smoke, stay low, on your hands and knees if necessary, to avoid being overcome by smoke and deadly gases and feel your way to the exit.

Be alert for a possible rescue attempt. Should you hear noises outside the aircraft, don't tip off the terrorists by staring out the window or staring in the direction of the noise. Get down in your seat and be ready to cover your head or shield your children.

Once the rescue effort is initiated, don't get involved. Assume that the rescuers are professionals and know what they are doing. Just follow orders. Whatever you do, don't pick up a stray weapon. The rescuers will probably shoot anyone with a gun.

Be on the lookout for terrorists who try to blend in with the passengers once the shooting starts. One of the terrorists involved in the hijacking of the EgyptAir flight to Malta attempted to escape by posing as a passenger. Until the situation is under control, the rescuers are likely to treat you and the other passengers roughly. You may even be frisked. This is a wise precaution on their part, and you should not be offended.

Don't be surprised if you are beset by psychological problems in the aftermath of a hijacking ordeal. This is normal. Most hostages suffer from at least some postcrisis psychological problems. Some survivors relate that they feel guilty over having been the focus of so much concern. Others are tormented by feelings that they did not do enough to resist or that they were somehow collaborators. It is not unusual for hostages who behaved in a cool and exemplary fashion during the ordeal to fall apart later, when they no longer need to be tough. There is no shame in seeking counseling and professional help if you need it.

Remember that such crises may have a greater impact on your family than on you. They also may need counseling.

Visiting Third World Countries

Use a world-band radio. It is a good idea to carry a world-band radio in Third World countries to monitor the international news and local developments. Remember, in most Third World countries, the media are controlled by the state and you cannot depend on the information you receive.

Carry a candle or a small flashlight. Power outages are common in many Third World nations, so you will appreciate having a source of light.

Carry a multilingual card with your blood type and any allergic reactions to medications.

Always know how to use the local telephones and carry appropriate change.

Staying in Hotels

If possible, consider checking in under another name. Accommodating hotels regularly accord this privilege to celebrities to help preserve their privacy. You can tell anyone you are expecting to hear from to ask for you by your pseudonym when he or she is trying to get in touch with you. This also will help the hotel screen your telephone calls.

Unfortunately, hotels in many Third World countries, and even those in Western European nations such as France, require that you give them your passport when checking in. Thus, you may be prevented from registering under another name unless the local authorities give their approval to the hotel.

Watch out for eavesdroppers. Hotel operators often eavesdrop on conversations, as all calls generally go through the switchboard, even if you dial the call yourself. Be cautious about what you say on the phone.

Don't stay on the ground level. Rooms on the ground level are generally far more vulnerable to attack than those on upper levels. Alternatively, don't stay in a room that is beyond the reach of fire engine ladders.

Pay attention to who occupies surrounding rooms. Be careful about who occupies the rooms above and below you, as well as those on either side. In addition, rooms with suspended ceilings may conceal all sorts of surprises.

Avoid rooms that share balconies with others. Older buildings also may be located so close to their neighbors that your window is only a few feet from another window or a rooftop. In such cases, it is best to request another room.

In communist countries, assume that your room is bugged. This is true in many Third World countries as well. Most major Intourist hotels in the Soviet Union have bugs that can be activated in any room. If you must talk confidentially, turn up the radio or television or run the water in the bathroom and converse in a low voice. A child's "magic pad," which erases all writing when you pull up the top sheet, is very handy for writing out conversations with another person. After using the magic pad, make certain it is secured, since it is possible to reconstruct what you have written from the wax backing.

Remember, however, that your room also may be under visual surveillance. Advances in fiber optics now mean that a tiny camera lens, no bigger than a wire, can be embedded in the wall to transmit pictures into another room.

If it's hot, don't touch it. In the case of a fire alarm, assume it is the real thing. Never open a door before determining whether flames are on the other side. Feel the doorknob and door; if they are hot, don't open the door. Search for some other avenue of escape.

Be prepared in case of a fire. Most nations do not require sprinkler systems and abundant exits in hotels. Given the rash of major high-rise hotel fires in developing countries in recent years, you may want to consider carrying a small rope ladder in your luggage. In the event that you are trapped in your room by approaching flames, you can dangle the ladder from your window and escape to a lower floor.

Should you have to throw on clothes to evacuate a burning hotel, grab clothing made of natural fibers. Polyester garments melt to the skin and provide less protection.

Learn if someone has been in your room in your absence. If you want to learn if someone was in your room (other than the maid), leave a voice-activated tape recorder in a drawer, cracked slightly so as not to muffle the sound.

Beware of approaching your room if people are loitering outside. Also, be wary of people who ride the elevator with you and get off on the same floor.

Socializing and Exchanging Money

If you are invited to a large social function, you might want to ask what security measures have been taken. Obviously, "invitation only" functions tend to be safer than those open to the general public. You also might want to know the names of others who will be at the function, since high-profile guests might attract attacks that could catch you in the cross fire. Be especially careful about functions that receive a great deal of advance publicity.

When abroad, select your restaurants and clubs carefully and try to maintain a low profile. Terrorists frequently target popular tourist haunts and places where American citizens are known to congregate, so be wary about going to these places.

Be careful when exchanging money. Generally, wherever you travel, you must exchange your dollars for francs, pesos, rubles, or whatever the local currency is. Unless you speak the local language and know your way around the country, you should exchange your dollars at a bank or other official currency exchange, despite the fact that you can often get a much more favorable exchange rate on the black market (unofficial). Some countries take a dim view of black market currency transactions, and if you are caught, you could land in a very unpleasant foreign jail. Moreover, exchanging a large wad of cash on the black market is always tricky and often dangerous. Some Americans have received counterfeit local currency. Others have been mugged after completing their transactions, presumably by the same individuals with whom they just did business. Still others have been arrested by local police in what amounts to a setup and then forced to pay a large bribe to escape criminal charges. If you are intent on using the black market as your banker, consider hiring a trusted local person to conduct the transaction on your behalf.

Understand the use of bribes. Bribes, or baksheesh, are common throughout the world, especially in Third World countries. You cannot avoid paying a little money to grease the bureaucracy in some places, so don't be shocked if it takes a bribe to get expedited through customs, to obtain a good hotel room, or even to make a telephone call. This author knows of one African country where it takes a few coins to pass through a military checkpoint or to motivate some police officers controlling the traffic lights to turn them from red to green.

Learn to live with petty graft if you plan on being an adventurous traveler or if you do business in the Third World. If you are involved in business abroad, remember that in some places it is necessary to pay off local officials and functionaries if you want anything done, including things such as having your phones hooked up, obtaining work permits for your employees, and renting office space.

On a large scale, paying bribes to foreign officials to obtain contracts and business agreements is prohibited by the Foreign Corrupt Practices Act, but submitting to petty corruption is unavoidable. It does you little good to complain, and if you refuse to oblige those on the take, they can make it all but impossible for you to do business in their country.

Always be discreet when offering a bribe. For example, if the desk clerk says there are no rooms at the hotel or you want a better room, lay your passport down on the counter with a $20 bill protruding from it. You may be surprised at how quickly the desk clerk will discover a vacancy. On the outside chance that he or she complains that you are offering a bribe, simply deny the accusation and maintain that the $20 bill must have gotten stuck inadvertently in your passport.

3

Nightlife

Let's begin with the observation that those who go looking for trouble generally find it. I do not recommend that you indulge in illicit pleasures such as gambling, drugs, or prostitution, but experience suggests that many people, despite the risks, do so. This chapter is designed to help you minimize the personal risks involved, especially when you are traveling in a foreign country.

Adult Entertainment Districts

Adult entertainment districts are usually located in the seedier, and therefore more dangerous, parts of town. If you must venture out after dark in search of fun, heed these basic precautions.

If possible, don't go by yourself. There is safety in numbers.

Dress in casual clothing. Don't wear an expensive suit and make sure you leave your jewelry, passport, and anything else you don't want to lose at the hotel in a safe deposit box.

Hire a car and driver. Don't rely on taxicabs. Taxis may be scarce late at night when you are ready to return to your hotel. Moreover, if you are inebriated, the taxi driver may attempt to roll or overcharge you. A driver procured through your hotel is much more likely to be reliable and trustworthy. He also will probably know the more reputable places to go and can prevent you from straying into a clip joint.

Hire a bodyguard. In some Third World countries, it is not a bad idea to hire a bodyguard for the evening.

Prostitutes

Carry only the necessary amount of cash. Determine in advance approximately how much you intend to pay and carry only that amount. Leave the rest at your hotel. You will not only be in a better bargaining position ("See, I have only this much"), but if you are rolled, you will lose less.

Agree on a price in advance. Repeat the price so that there will be no misunderstanding. Some hookers will threaten to cause a scene in order to extract more money from you. Even the finest hotels are skilled in dealing with hookers, so don't hesitate to ask the night manager (and the hotel security staff) for assistance. You can rely on their discretion, especially if you offer them a tip later for their understanding.

Don't try to cheat a hooker. Prostitutes may act submissive when the meter is running, but woe to anyone who tries to cheat them. He may be slashed with a razor or assaulted by the woman's pimp.

Never give the hooker your real name. Alternatively, use only your first name. On the one hand, some experts say that you should never take a hooker back to your hotel room or apartment, as this invites trouble. On the other hand, your hotel is the safest place for a tryst.

Make sure you choose the place. Never let the hooker lead you anywhere or have you drive her to a spot of her choosing.

She may have accomplices waiting to roll you or worse. Try to avoid fleabag hotels and places that charge by the hour.

Select a high-quality brothel. Patronizing a high-quality, and therefore generally more expensive, brothel or escort service is always preferable to picking up a bar girl or streetwalker. Most brothel operators are required to scrutinize the health of their employees and offer a generally safe environment for patrons. Some tony London brothels, for example, offer a high degree of security and cleanliness.

Be careful when cruising for sex. If you are cruising a red-light district in a car, never let the prostitute get into the car to discuss business. It may be difficult, and possibly dangerous, to eject her if you cannot come to terms. Also beware of female gangs that lure potential customers over to the curb ostensibly to bargain about the price and then mug them.

Double pleasure can be double trouble. Never take those two-for-one deals. When you get the women back to the room, one may rifle through your pockets while the other is taking you around the world.

Drink in moderation. You are an easy mark if you don't have your wits about you. Contrary to what some people believe, alcohol will not sharpen your senses, quicken your reflexes, or improve your aim. It will only give you a false sense of security and slow you down in an emergency.

Never let the hooker pay the bar bill. This is a great way to end up with a $400 tab. It is amazing how many individuals, with too many drinks under their belt, actually give the hookers their wallet and ask them to take care of the bill. You run the risk of their absconding with your wallet, reading your identification cards and learning where you live, or stealing a few banknotes or credit cards.

Ask the concierge to make all of the necessary arrangements. In many better European hotels, the concierge will take care of all the financial arrangements and have a hooker known to the establishment discreetly brought to your room.

Practice safe sex. A much higher ratio of prostitutes test positive for the AIDS virus than do people in the general population. This is attributable both to their high number of sexual partners and the fact that many are intravenous drug users. Prostitutes also are often carriers of venereal diseases. Thus, you are clearly taking an enormous risk by engaging a prostitute. Whatever you do, practice safe sex: Use a condom.

To reduce the incidence of venereal disease, prostitutes in many countries must submit to a weekly health checkup, after which they receive a certificate stating that they are clean. Bar owners and houses of prostitution are forbidden to let them work if they don't receive a clean bill of health. If you know which day of the week they are examined, you can lessen your exposure by contracting their services later that same day. Remember, however, that a prostitute is only as clean as the last person she or he has serviced.

Stay out of trouble by avoiding it. The reason many individuals seek out prostitutes and raunchy nightclubs is loneliness and boredom. When planning a business trip, arrange in advance to spend your evenings with old friends or business associates, thereby reducing your free time. Also consider bringing your spouse along.

Alcohol and Drugs

Guard against intestinal disorders. In most Third World countries, don't drink the water, even if it is combined with alcohol. The alcohol will not kill the germs. Also beware of mixers that the bartender has made using tap water. Similarly, ice cubes made from tap water also can make you sick. Stick to wine, beer, and drinks made with bottled mixers.

Beware of being slipped a Mickey. In many seedy bars, the bartender may slip something in your drink to disorient you or make you drowsy. Afterward, you will be rolled and dumped in the alley, poorer and usually much the worse for wear. To guard against this possibility, forgo mixed drinks and take beer or wine by the bottle. Ask that the bottle be opened at the table in front of you.

Beware of clip joints. In such establishments, friendly bar girls will ask you to buy them drinks, often overpriced champagne by the bottle. Once you stop buying, they will lose interest in you, and you are likely to be stuck with an exorbitant bar bill. If you object too vigorously, the bouncer is likely to strong-arm you.

Expect the worst when purchasing or using illegal drugs. While illegal drugs are available in virtually every nation, including the Soviet Union and countries in Eastern Europe, you are running a grave risk by attempting to purchase them in an unfamiliar land. If you don't know the country and its language, you are more likely to get stung or arrested than in the United States. If you are arrested, don't expect to have access to a lawyer or to be granted your civil rights. You may be held incommunicado for a long period of time. You may be beaten by authorities trying to extract a confession. You may be held in a cold and filthy cell and subjected to sexual abuse by other inmates. In short, expect the worst.

Possession of even a small amount of narcotics can result in a protracted sentence, even life imprisonment. In one North African country, a young American was arrested for possession of less than a kilo of hashish. He was tried, convicted, and sentenced to ten years in prison. To discourage escape attempts, he was regularly beaten on the soles of his feet with a rubber truncheon. The U.S. government could do nothing except indicate its concern over his treatment.

Be aware that drugs in some countries are purer than those in the United States. In many countries, especially in Asia, narcotics are not cut as much as they are in the United States. Thus, doses are much stronger. You may not be used to such potent substances and can become dependent in a shorter period of time or even overdose. Moreover, if you are visiting a nation in which drugs are plentiful and relatively cheap, resist the temptation to do too much. This is a sure formula for disaster.

Don't travel with drugs. Possession of controlled substances is a crime nearly everywhere in the world. In this era of international terrorism, traveling with drugs is downright foolish. You never know when you will be subjected to a pat-down search or required to open your baggage. Even a minute amount of marijuana discovered in your possession at an airport security checkpoint may result in your being arrested on the spot and taken to jail.

Check for smuggling of drugs on corporate aircraft and yachts. Your security staff should regularly inspect your corporate aircraft or yacht to ensure that drugs are not being smuggled on board by the crew or a member of the maintenance staff. Should U.S. Customs officials discover even a small amount of a controlled substance, they may detain or arrest all on board and confiscate the aircraft or yacht. At the very least, you may miss a critical business meeting and be the subject of unfavorable publicity.

Never carry a suitcase or unopened parcel abroad for a friend. It may contain drugs or some other proscribed or controlled substance. Your protests that you didn't know what was inside are likely to fall on deaf ears.

Gambling

Get rid of that thick roll of bills. Don't travel to the rough part of town with a great deal of visible cash. At the very least, spread it around in many pockets.

If you must carry cash to gamble, carry most of it tucked down in your socks, in a money belt, or in your underwear. You will have access to it, but it will be more discreet.

Gamble at a hotel or other respectable establishment. Beware of seedy gambling halls and out-of-the-way gaming spots. Not only is the house less likely to pay off at such places, but should you win big, you might have trouble leaving with your winnings. Games are less likely to be rigged at a major hotel or tourist spot.

Don't gamble and drink heavily. Drinking not only compounds the odds against your winning, but it also makes you vulnerable to thugs and prostitutes who cruise gambling halls looking for an inebriated mark to roll. Resist the free drinks proffered by gambling establishments to keep you playing and impair your judgment.

Beware of shill games. Gambling establishments, especially those featuring card games, abound with hucksters offering "foolproof" ways to beat the house or take a third party. Often the third party is a shill, and you are the one who is being set up. In addition, if you are caught trying to cheat the house, you could end up in an alley fighting for your life.

Avoid cockfights, dogfights, and other illegal betting games. Such games may be raided by the police. Even in some Third World countries, you run the risk of a police raid, although it may be for the purpose of shaking you down for a bribe to keep you out of jail.

General Social Tips

Know the culture of the country you are visiting. Many seemingly innocent habits and actions on your part may offend people of other cultures.

Don't play the joker. A laugh may be good for breaking the ice, but don't overdo it. A funnyman often finds that the joke is on him. People may take offense at his remarks, or they may misconstrue a joke aimed at them. Horseplay in a bar can easily turn nasty. For instance, an offhand remark by a former CIA officer in a Latin American bar resulted in the man's death. He called another patron a *maricon* (queer) and was knifed in the stomach.

Avoid being the Ugly American. Don't apply U.S. standards to food, service, cleanliness, and accommodations. In many countries, especially Third World countries, things are not the same, and no amount of complaining will correct them. Avoid making unfavorable comparisons with the United States. Roll with the punches and take the rest of the world on its own terms.

Don't feel you have to adopt all the local habits and vices. Just because the local executives frequent prostitutes or use drugs doesn't mean you have to do these things to get along. You will win their respect by maintaining your dignity and doing only those things that are consistent with your own values and morals.

You will not enjoy much popularity, however, if you are extremely judgmental and outspoken about local behavior that is inconsistent with your own values and morals. Make your point simply by not participating.

4

Automobile Security

At no time are you more vulnerable than when traveling in your automobile or getting in or out of it. In more than 80 percent of all assassination and kidnapping attacks, the victim is targeted while riding in his car or while in close proximity to it. Among those killed in transit were former president John F. Kennedy, Dominican Republic strongman Raphael Trujillo, United Nations (UN) mediator Count Folke Bernadotte, Nazi reichsprotector Reinhard Heydrich, Spanish prime minister Luis Carrero Blanco, former Nicaraguan dictator Anastasio Somoza, Nigerian president Brigadier General Murtalla Mohammed, British ambassador to Ireland Christopher Ewart-Briggs, former Chilean cabinet minister Orlando Letelier, Austrian archduke Francis Ferdinand (whose death precipitated World War I), and, most recently, Colombia's attorney general. The leader of Italy's Christian Democrats, Aldo Moro, and West German industrialist Hans Martin Schleyer were killed after being abducted from their automobiles. French president Charles de Gaulle, Jordan's King Hussein, former NATO commander General Alexander Haig, East German leader Erich Honecker, Prime Minister Robert Mugabe of Zimbabwe, and U.S. secretary of state George Shultz have all survived assassination attempts that occurred while they were traveling by car. Finally, President Ronald Reagan was only a few steps from his limousine when he was shot by John Hinckley, Jr.

Thus, it is vital to your security that you take every reasonable precaution to ensure your safety during automobile travel. In addition, it is important that your vehicle be properly secured when it is not in use to prevent sabotage.

Equipment

The vehicle itself. It is unlikely that you will ever be involved in a high-speed car chase. Instead of a very fast vehicle, I suggest you select a very robust vehicle. A four-wheel-drive vehicle such as a Jeep, Blazer, Bronco, Ranger, or Landcruiser will give you the ground clearance and traction necessary to circumvent obstacles flanked by ditches or high curbs. It also has the power to ram through a barricade.

Should you want your vehicle hardened, or armored, vehicles such as those listed above possess the power and reinforced suspension to carry the extra load. They also may be the best value for the money. In some Third World countries, such vehicles are classified as farm equipment and are not subject to the same high importation taxes as luxury cars.

If you prefer a traditional automobile to one of the vehicles noted above, avoid driving a flashy sports car or luxury car (such as a Cadillac, Lincoln, or Mercedes Benz). Such cars call attention to your wealth and position and are easy to follow. Select a vehicle that blends into your surroundings and is painted a neutral color.

Mandatory equipment. Beware of purchasing unnecessary extras. Many gadgets on the market are just that, gadgets. Some may actually increase your risk. Mandatory equipment includes a heavy-duty or reinforced front bumper and skid plates to protect your oil pan and differentials. Your gasoline tank should either be surrounded by armor or be self-sealing, with antiexplosive baffles inside. A second fuel tank also might come in handy, but it will add weight to an already heavy vehicle.

You might want to consider beefing up your vehicle's transmission. Limited slip differentials will help you get out of a rut, while a gear ratio sufficient for towing a trailer will give you quicker acceleration.

Make certain that your car will not die on you. A larger battery (or second battery), heavy-duty alternator, and beefed-up cooling system are all important options, especially in extreme climates.

Radio or telephone. Some kind of communications system is a must so that you can call for help and your office and security people can stay in touch with you. So as not to call attention to your vehicle, buy an antenna that wraps around the interior of the roof or is hidden in the window post or side mirror. Some two-way radio antennas can be disguised to look like ordinary AM/FM radio antennas.

Make certain that your communications system is flexible and reliable and will work in its intended environment. Remember, tall buildings, forests, and hills cut down on your transmission and reception ability.

First aid kit. Carry a first aid kit, especially in Third World countries, where medical attention in an emergency might not be readily available. Some experts recommend a trauma kit for treating gunshot and shrapnel wounds. If you have a chauffeur, consider having him trained in cardiopulmonary resuscitation (CPR) and first aid.

Locking gas cap. A locking gas cap will keep contaminants and explosives out of your tank. One note of caution: In cold climates, locking gas caps can freeze. Squirt some oil in them before the onset of winter to prevent this from happening.

Fire extinguisher. Carry a fire extinguisher in your vehicle and insist that it be inspected on a regular basis to ensure that it works properly.

Air conditioner. An air conditioner will keep you from having to drive with an open window in warm climates. Since most bulletproof windows will not roll down because of their thickness, an air conditioner is a must if you are going to install bulletproof glass.

Door locks. Childproof door locks will keep an intruder from popping them with a coat hanger. A central locking system also is handy.

Other Accessories

Lights. High-intensity lights mounted on your front bumper or in your grille will give you additional visibility at night, as will a side- or top-mounted spotlight. A set of halogen lamps aimed backward can be used to blind anyone pursuing you. A pulsating high-intensity light mounted on top of the car will make it more difficult for a sniper to get a clear shot at night.

Night vision equipment. Although night vision goggles are rather exotic, they will permit you to drive without lights in order to escape pursuit.

Alarms. A variety of alarms are available to tell you if someone is tampering with your vehicle.

Fire-retardant systems. A common method of stopping vehicles is with fire. Molotov cocktails can be hurled at a vehicle, and burning barricades can be used to trap a vehicle. Even if the vehicle doesn't catch fire, Molotov cocktails can blacken the windshield (preventing further maneuvering) or invade the air intakes with noxious, even toxic, fumes. You may want to install a fire-suppression system that will flood the exterior with various fire retardants. Similarly, you should consider placing air intakes so that they are not vulnerable to fumes.

Tear gas dispensers. In countries where mob violence is common, tear gas dispensers can be hidden in your car's body to prevent hostile crowds from tipping the car over or trying to assault it. Such devices are often concealed in the fender wells. Your vehicle will have to be sealed to ensure that the tear gas does not invade the car's interior. You also might want to have gas masks for the passengers inside the car.

Sirens. Experience has demonstrated that piercing sirens or air horns may confuse, frighten, and disorient attackers. A siren also calls attention to the vehicle if it is under attack and may summon police. If you are being pursued, it also can be used to clear the road in front of you.

Loudspeakers. A microphone connected to an outside loudspeaker will enable you to communicate with those outside the car without having to open your doors or windows.

Vanity plates. Whatever you do, don't succumb to the temptation to advertise your identity by purchasing vanity license plates. Plates that call attention to your profession or your company name simply increase your vulnerability.

Remote control starters. There are several reliable remote control starters on the market. They permit you to start your car from a safe distance, a good precaution in countries where terrorists are known to rig bombs in parked cars. Nevertheless, a remote control starter is by no means infallible. In Northern Ireland, for example, terrorists build bombs that are not activated until the car is in motion.

Exhaust pipes. Consider putting bolts through the end of your vehicle's exhaust pipe to prevent anyone from inserting an alien object, such as an explosive device.

To Armor or Not to Armor

Pros and cons. Armoring, or hardening, your vehicle will certainly afford you greater protection, but the decision to purchase an armored vehicle involves a number of considerations. First, armored vehicles are very expensive, running into the hundreds of thousands of dollars. Second, armoring is heavy and reduces the gas mileage and maneuverability of your vehicle. For every increase in weight, expect a proportional decrease in speed. The added weight also will place additional strain on your vehicle's engine and suspension. Third, an armored car is not a tank. Armor may defeat small arms fire and some rocket-propelled grenades, but it will not defend you against many weapons available to terrorists today. Antitank weapons, after all, are designed to destroy battle tanks, and nothing you slap on your sedan can defeat them. Similarly, armor will not defeat all land mines and cache bombs buried in the road.

The level of armor protection. The purchase of an armored car should be made with the assistance of a knowledgeable security consultant. Once the consultant understands the level of the threat to you, he or she can match the appropriate armor to your situation.

Armor is rated according to an Underwriter's Laboratory grading system. Level II will stop, for example, a .357-magnum or 9-mm handgun. Level III will defeat a .44-magnum, 12-gauge shotgun, or .30-caliber carbine round. Level IV is designed to stop a 30.06 military ball round.

Ballistic testing is done on a VBL scale. V50BL means that at a given velocity and range, a given round has a 50 percent chance of penetrating the armor in question. V0BL, on the other hand, indicates that the armor has a 100 percent probability of defeating the round in question. Use that as your standard.

Hardened steel still provides the best protection, as plastic laminates tend to break up under repeated hits. The disadvantage of steel is its weight. Since presumably you will attempt to defeat an ambush by driving through it or racing away from it, you may want to opt for a lighter, cheaper, more maneuverable vehicle. During the past quarter century, new lightweight materials such as Kevlar, a fiberglass and resin compound that was developed during the Vietnam War, have revolutionized the armored car business, providing maximum protection with only a marginal increase in weight.

The purchase. Guard against unscrupulous salesmen just as you would terrorists. Watch out for security consultants who are shills for particular companies. Beware of manufacturers that make misleading or bogus claims. Armor that can stop bullets at 100 yards may be worthless if a terrorist attacks at point-blank range. Note that .45-caliber bullets are often easier to deflect than high-velocity, full-jacketed 9-mm parabellum or .357- or .44-magnum rounds.

Most armorers ask that you deal directly with them so they can build your vehicle to your exact needs and specifications. This author sees no reason for using a middleman and urges you to deal directly with the firm that will armor your vehicle. Most will purchase the basic vehicle for you and then modify it.

Note that a number of armorers go out of business each year. The reasons vary, but the most common causes are unreliable products, exaggerated claims, poor servicing, and overpricing. As with any expensive purchase, especially one on which your life may depend, you and your security chief (or adviser) should go over the manufacturer's background. Ask to check with some of his previous clients to see how satisfied they are with his products and servicing.

Before signing a contract, insist on a test firing at the armor plate, and have it done at close range. Demand that at any stage in the construction of your vehicle, your representatives be allowed to remove a section of the armor to conduct additional test firings. Also insist on your right to inspect the vehicle during construction to verify the quality of the workmanship. You should expect complete confidentiality from your armorer. The fewer people who know specifics about your security the better. Your armorer should not use your name or that of your company in his promotional activities without your permission.

Quality control. You and your security chief should go over the placement of the armor. Remember, the fire wall must be armored against rounds fired obliquely at the passenger compartment through the front fenders. You also might want to armor the undercarriage and roof of the vehicle to afford greater protection against mines and grenades.

Pay special attention to how the windows are fitted and to the quality of the bullet-resistant glass. Like armor, bullet-resistant glass—usually layered glass with a layer of transparent polycarbonate in the middle—comes in various strengths. Because of its weight and thickness, door and window frames generally must be reinforced and widened.

All brake and fuel lines should be moved behind the armor. You also should scrutinize the way the steering, brakes, and suspension system must be beefed up to accommodate the extra weight. Your vehicle should be able to handle the extra weight of the armor, together with passengers and luggage, with power to spare. A car that lacks acceleration and has to labor up hills may become a death trap.

General Precautions

Vary your routine. This is perhaps the most important security rule of all. The underlying reason for virtually every successful attack on someone traveling by car is that the person was predictable. Whatever you do, try *not* to be predictable. Do not make the terrorist's job easy. Vary your route to and from work, vary the time you leave in the morning and come home in the evening, and vary your route to and from routine destinations.

If there is only one access road to and from your house or office, exercise particular caution in those areas. Be alert for signs of trouble or anything that looks suspicious.

Use common sense. Just as there are areas you probably avoid in any major U.S. city, the same holds true elsewhere. By staying out of the bad part of town, you limit your vulnerability to both terrorism and ordinary street crime. Watch out for people who approach you when you are stopped at a traffic light. Beware of people who flag you down for assistance.

A common trick in Colombia, for example, is for a child to approach a car stopped at a traffic light with the window rolled down. The child will grab the driver's watch, which is usually worn on the left arm. On the passenger side of the car, the thief will sometimes stab at the victim's hand with a knife or burning cigar. When the victim reaches over to grab the injured hand or to block the attacker, the thief will tear the watch off the left wrist.

Exercise caution in parking. Never park your vehicle in an unsecure area. Never routinely park your vehicle in the same place. As a rule, you should not have an assigned parking space at your place of work; try to park in a different spot every day. Never put your name on your parking spot; there is safety in remaining anonymous.

Always inspect your vehicle before getting in it (see the next item). If you return to your vehicle and find it has a flat tire, be on your guard. Someone may have cut the tire in order to jump you while you are replacing it.

If your chauffeur-driven vehicle is parked in its usual spot but the chauffeur is nowhere to be seen, suspect foul play. Do not sit in the vehicle waiting for the chauffeur to return; you may get another driver not to your liking.

Check for bombs. Before getting in your vehicle, check it carefully for signs of tampering, which could mean that a bomb has been placed on board. Look for tape or scuff marks, packages or trash around the vehicle, protruding wires or string, ground disturbed beneath the vehicle, foreign objects inside or attached to the vehicle, or anything else that looks out of place. If you suspect something but can't find a bomb, don't get in your vehicle. Repeat: Don't get in it. Alert the authorities immediately and see that a thorough inspection is undertaken:

- Survey the exterior of the car for anything unusual.
- Look inside for foreign objects or anything that doesn't appear right.
- Check the wheel wells.
- Pay particular attention to the spot where the tires make contact with the ground and check for pressure-release firing devices there.
- Check for anything in your exhaust pipe(s).
- Look underneath the vehicle. Has the ground been disturbed? Have any foreign objects, such as a soap dish, been attached to the undercarriage?
- Open the trunk and examine the contents for anything that doesn't belong there.
- Check the gas tank and cap for signs of tampering. Be sure to have a lock on your gas cap.
- Inspect the grille and bumpers.
- Lift the hood and examine the engine compartment carefully.
- Open the doors after examining them carefully and inspect the interior of the vehicle, especially beneath the seats, on the floor, and under the dash. Also check behind the visors, the headrests, and the glove compartment.
- Check the spare tire for explosives hidden inside it.

Don't trust valet parking attendants. Give a valet parking attendant only your vehicle key, never your entire set of keys.

Some cars have a "chauffeur's key" that will operate only the ignition and not unlock the trunk or glove compartment. Always keep your glove compartment and trunk locked. Do not leave any papers in the car that identify you, your residence, or your place of work. Make a point of noting your odometer reading in the valet's presence; this may deter him from taking your car for a joyride.

Be especially wary when entering or exiting your vehicle. This is your most vulnerable moment. If you can avoid it, never enter or exit your car in the open. Ideally, you should do so only in a sheltered area, such as an underground garage. Today, if the president has to enter or exit his vehicle in a public place, a portable tent is set up to shield him from view.

Always take stock of your surroundings. If something does not look right, abort your trip and alert your security. A kidnapping or assassination attempt will usually be preceded by a period during which you are under surveillance. Be alert to any individual or vehicle you encounter frequently; it may not be coincidence.

Avoid narrow, congested streets. Think ambush. On the way to the office, instead of playing a tape or the radio, planning your day, or mulling over your work, create a scenario to kidnap yourself. Think of how you would do it. Which part of your route leaves you most vulnerable? What do you see around you that an abductor might use for cover or to slow you down? Traffic jams, drawbridges, any area where the road narrows, and places where buildings and culverts on either side limit your maneuverability are prime ambush sites. Try to stay on main streets where the traffic generally moves smoothly.

You will no doubt think of other danger zones. Any area that restricts your mobility (congested areas, steep hills, intersections, traffic signals, or railroad tracks) or any area that allows an assailant to get close to you unobserved (bridges over the roadway or extensive shrubbery near the road) should trigger a danger signal in your head. Former Nigerian president Murtalla Mohammed was assassinated because he got caught in the same traffic jam at the same time every day on the way to the presidential palace.

When driving on a freeway, try to use the inside lane near the center of the road. It is much easier to force a car over or to pull up on the driver's side when you are hugging the right lane.

Beware of motorcycles. Many assassins ride motorcycles to escape more easily through heavy traffic after an attack. Be cautious of motorcycles pulling up alongside your vehicle, especially when there are two riders with darkened full-face visors. Remember, they can hide in your vehicle's blind spot near the right rear fender.

Keep your distance at traffic lights. When stopped at a traffic light, do not pull abreast of another vehicle so that your window is opposite the other vehicle's. Do not pull up so close to the bumper of the car in front of you that you cannot move. Stop well back, allowing enough space in front so that you can drive out to either side if necessary.

Be especially watchful in rural areas and at night. In many foreign countries, especially in the Third World, rural driving and darkness magnify your risk significantly. In places such as Jamaica, Zaire, Mexico, Lebanon, and Uganda, thugs armed with automatic weapons often set up roadblocks and demand money for passage. Sometimes they simply murder motorists and take their cars. Consider traveling in lonely rural areas only if you must, and then by convoy if at all possible.

Keep an eye on your driver. Make certain that he stays alert. Point out to him that he will be of no use to terrorists and probably shot in the initial moments of an ambush. Screen your driver's background and make certain that he does not have weaknesses that would make it easy for potential kidnappers to compromise him, such as excessive drinking, drugs, gambling, or deviant sexual practices. There are many cases on record in which the chauffeur either sold information to terrorists regarding his boss's schedule or actually assisted in planning the kidnapping.

Remember, the chauffeur's principal job is to drive, not to shoot it out with terrorists. He should keep both hands on the wheel, concentrate on escape and evasion, and use his gun, if he has one, only as a last resort. Moreover, if he has a gun, he should be well trained in its use and required to meet certain minimum standards on a regular basis.

Always wear your seat belt or, preferably, a shoulder harness. Not only will this cut down the likelihood of your being seriously injured in an automobile crash, but you need to be well anchored to perform many of the demanding maneuvers cited below.

Always travel with your doors locked. Your windows also should be closed, requiring air-conditioning in warm or tropical climates.

Take an evasive or aggressive driving course. Terrorists will usually try to ambush you when you are stalled in traffic or can be barricaded on a narrow street. Thus, movements such as the bootlegger's turn are not likely to be of any help, since they require plenty of room and high speed. You and your chauffeur should, however, know how to perform a reverse 180 and to ram obstacles out of your way.

To execute a reverse 180, slow to a stop by pumping lightly on your brakes (slamming on the brakes causes you to skid). When the car comes to a stop and the weight of the car is distributed over the rear wheels, put the car in reverse and accelerate to fifteen to twenty miles per hour. Cross your left hand over to the lower right of the wheel, swing the wheel vigorously a half or three-quarter turn, and shift into drive as the car swings back around in the direction from which you just came. (Note: You cannot turn the wheel too hard or vigorously.) With the reverse 180, you are not swinging into danger but retreating from it.

For all its vulnerability, an automobile is a potent weapon that can be used to knock barricades out of your way. When ramming another vehicle, aim for the rear tire (you must hit the axle for the best result). The rear end is the lightest part of the vehicle, and a good hit will cause the car to swing out of your way. If circumstances require you to ram the front of the vehicle, do not hit any farther back than the front wheel.

When ramming your way through a barricade, prepare for a shock. You should already be strapped into your seat. Young children should be in a restraining harness. If neither you nor your child are prepared, throw your child to the floor and brace yourself against the steering wheel. If at all possible, make sure your windows are rolled up, since the windows of the car you are ramming often explode, causing glass to fly everywhere.

Never permit yourself to become boxed in. To guard against this possibility, never follow too closely behind another car. When stopping at a traffic signal, leave yourself enough space to maneuver. Keep your distance from traffic accidents and obstacles. If you see a problem in the road ahead, try to turn around or maneuver onto a side street to avoid it.

Whatever you do, don't stop. If you are under attack, you are generally safe as long as you keep moving. Try to flee the scene of the attack as quickly as possible. To this end, drive over curbs, lawns, sidewalks—anything—to get away. Do not try to fight your way out of the situation unless you have no other option.

Never leave your car unless it is moving more slowly than you can run.

Beware of obstacles in the road. Terrorists may attempt to block your vehicle with something such as a child's buggy. Don't hesitate to knock it out of the way if you have reason to believe you are under attack.

If you are a threatened person, never stop for what appears to be a traffic accident or other roadside incident. It may be a ruse to get you to pull over so you can be kidnapped. If you feel that you must do something, use the communications system in your vehicle to report the accident or drive to a police station. Never leave your car.

Also beware of policemen who try to flag down your car. The uniform you see may be counterfeit. By all means stop, but roll the window down only slightly, keep the car in gear, and be ready to speed away. Always ask the police officer for some kind of identification.

During a recent kidnapping in Europe, the victim's car was struck by another car during a rainstorm in what seemed, at first, to be an ordinary fender bender. When the victim got out to inspect the damage, he was approached by a uniformed policeman who suggested that they get in the backseat of the victim's car, out of the rain, where he would take the victim's statement. Once the victim was in the backseat with the policeman, another man jumped in on the other side and stuck a gun in the victim's ribs. A third accomplice climbed behind the wheel and drove the car away, with the victim effectively hemmed in by the men in the backseat.

Don't stop for a flat tire. Should terrorists place something in the road to puncture your tires, keep on going. If only one tire is deflated, the steering wheel will pull to one side, but with the adrenalin pumping through your veins, you should be able to maintain a straight course. Your flat tire may eventually catch fire if you are driving fast, so head for the nearest refuge.

You also can purchase "run flat," or compartmentalized, tires that will not deflate even after being struck by bullets. Such tires are, however, very expensive.

Weapons

Firearms. You can use your car to avoid or outrun attackers or even to run them down. But if you want some firepower for additional protection, consider a double-barreled shotgun (not less than an 18 1/4-inch barrel) or a 12-gauge pump riot gun loaded with .00 buckshot. Shotguns are easy to operate and, unlike pistols, don't require the same amount of practice. If you point the shotgun in approximately the right direction and pull the trigger, you are likely to hit something. Shotguns also are useful for their intimidation value.

Submachine guns also are effective in the close confines of a vehicle, but carbines and assault rifles may be unwieldy. Both submachine guns and sawed-off shotguns (under 16 inches), however, are generally illegal in the United States and feasible only in some dangerous parts of the Third World. Before purchasing any weapon, check with the authorities regarding local laws and licensing requirements.

While a pistol in the hands of an expert can be an extremely effective weapon, more than likely neither you nor your driver will devote enough time to pistol shooting to become experts. Thus, if you are armed solely with pistols, you probably will be outgunned by your attackers, and returning fire may actually endanger your lives. As noted earlier, the best strategy is always to concentrate on evasion and escape rather than shooting it out with your attackers.

Gun ports. Unless you have gun ports, you will have to open a door or roll down a window (if possible) to return hostile fire. The West German counterterrorist unit GSG-9 even has gun ports built into the windshields of some of its Mercedes Benz autos.

Storage. Never store your weapons in open view. They should be secured in racks under the dash or in the doors. Never store a weapon with a magazine in it unless you fear imminent attack. Keep the magazines nearby, ready to slap into the weapon at the first sign of trouble.

5

Residential Security

YOUR home may be your castle, but without the modern equivalent of a moat, it can be a very vulnerable place. Next to traveling by car, you are most vulnerable when at your residence. This is because an attacker ordinarily can case your home for days to discover its vulnerabilities and anticipate the hours when you will be there. It is no accident that Israeli commandos killed top PLO official Abu Jihad in his home in Tunis and not somewhere else.

If you are a threatened person or live in a dangerous country, the addition of an alarm system or watchman is unlikely to provide you with adequate protection from all potential threats. It is not necessary that you turn your residence into a bunker to ensure your safety, but depending on your threat level, you should consider taking some, if not most, of the precautions listed below.

Choosing a House

Check with local police before you select a house. They can inform you about the crime rate in a particular neighborhood.

When selecting a residence, look for the following things:

- ✓ Good neighborhood
- ✓ Clearly visible approaches

- ✓ Off-street parking
- ✓ Multiple access routes
- ✓ High wall or fence
- ✓ Good exterior lighting
- ✓ Heavy-duty doors with peepholes
- ✓ Chains and strong locks on all doors
- ✓ Reliable alarm system
- ✓ Locks and metal grating on all skylights
- ✓ Some kind of window treatment on all ground-floor windows

Choose your neighbors. If at all possible, choose neighbors with a similar economic status and level of authority. Chances are that they will take security as seriously as you do and will be alert to strangers casing the neighborhood. The precautions they take to secure their own homes, such as exterior lighting, will make your own security tasks much easier.

If you are living abroad, you might want to live among other Americans, who usually can be found clustered in their own communities. Such a community will provide you with a ready source of friends who can be trusted. Any terrorist group trying to infiltrate the neighborhood will stand out. If you live in an American ghetto, however, your neighborhood and everyone in it may become targets of terrorists or hostile mobs simply because you are the most visible American presence in the area.

Choose a house that will allow you safe passage to and from work. In other words, pick a house that does not force you to drive through dangerous sections of the city and that allows you to vary your route to and from work.

Pay attention to terrain. In selecting a home, beware of a house situated below a hill or street that permits easy observation of all that goes on. At the same time, note that slight rises on your property may shield your house from attack from the street. Check the approaches to your property for drainage ditches and other areas that could conceal a sniper or provide cover for an intruder. Have such areas filled if possible, or install bright lighting and sensors.

Install fences. Consider circling your property with two tall chain-link fences separated by a gravel path wide enough for a man to pass through. The interior fence could be electrified if there are no small children or pets on your property. At the very least, intrusion detection sensors should be mounted on the fences and placed in the pathway. Closed-circuit television cameras can be placed looking down each pathway or corridor between the fences (there should be no blind spots), and bright lights should be installed to illuminate each pathway. The top of the fence should be strung with barbed, razor, or coiled concertina wire.

Some experts prefer a dark perimeter because intruders don't know what awaits them. They recommend infrared illuminators together with infrared-sensitive cameras. Although the grounds are dark to the naked eye, they are bright as day to someone watching the monitor.

If your home already has a high wall, you can embed sensors in it and top it with concertina wire or broken glass. Nevertheless, it should be combined with an interior fence constructed in the manner described previously.

All trees and poles that an intruder might scale to get over the fences should be cut down or moved. At the very least, overhanging branches should be pruned. Thick foliage outside the fence or on your grounds should be trimmed back so that it cannot conceal a sniper or intruder.

Install a gate that cannot be rammed through. Ideally, a security guard should man the gate twenty-four hours a day in a bulletproof guardhouse. If a security guard is impractical or too expensive, the gate can be activated by remote control from the house. Require that every guest or delivery person identify himself or herself from a phone box placed near the gate. Make certain that the gate area is brightly illuminated and swept with closed-circuit television cameras, including one camera positioned to identify the driver of any vehicle calling at the house. Any vehicle passing through the gate should be closely watched on the closed-circuit television screen to ensure that another vehicle or person on foot does not sneak in behind the authorized vehicle.

Consider purchasing guard dogs. You might want to consider having guard dogs roam your property, especially at night. With their keen sense of smell and excellent hearing, dogs are excellent alarm systems. However, do not expect a dog to fend off a determined intruder. Your canine sentry can be killed with a gun or a heavy stick or incapacitated with mace. Your dogs will, however, probably prevent you from being taken unawares and buy you valuable time to prepare to meet the attack. They also represent one more barrier that the intruder or terrorist will have to surmount before he can get to you.

When purchasing a dog, avoid the urge to get the meanest, most lethal type of attack dog available, such as a pit bull. Such dogs are often overbred and can turn on you, your family, or your friends. Do not purchase a walking time bomb or a lawsuit just waiting to happen. It is not a question of getting a big dog or a little dog but rather a very loud dog.

The U.S. Army is experimenting with geese as guard animals, since they are extremely alert and very noisy when disturbed. Peacocks are used for the same purpose in some countries.

Note: Sometimes a "Beware of Dog" sign is just as effective as the real thing, and, as one expert put it, you don't have to feed a sign.

Institute cooperative security. If you live among people you trust, integrate your security system with theirs. Trustworthy neighbors can watch your house while you are gone or summon police in an emergency. Get to know your neighbors and consider pooling your resources regarding things such as exterior lighting, block patrols, a common security force, and alarm systems.

Choosing Doors and Windows

Heavy doors. Steel doors are best, but heavy, solid wood doors also are acceptable if they are very thick and well made. The door frame is as important as the door and also should be made of steel. If your door is of the panel variety, the panels are often weak and can be kicked in with a heavy boot. Obviously, a door with a single-pane window is unlikely to provide a formidable obstacle to an intruder. Remember, the intruder has the initiative. He will select the weakest link in your defenses and attack there. In this connection, he will not be deterred by a solid steel front door if the rear door is wood and glass. Thus, your security must be comprehensive.

Door bolts. Your door bolts are vulnerable and should be protected. They should have something that protrudes from the door frame to keep tools such as a hacksaw or jimmy from being thrust in at the bolt.

If your door opens inward, the jamb of the door frame will protect the bolt. You may want to reinforce the jamb with a metal plate affixed to the frame. If your door opens outward, you should affix a flat metal plate called an escutcheon to it.

Door hinges. If your door opens outward, notice that the hinges are on the outside. An intruder may attempt to bypass your locks by taking the whole door off its hinges. Hinges on such doors should be nonremovable. Alternatively, you can fit a protruding screw to the door frame that will keep the door in place in case the hinge is undone.

Locks. A key-in-the-knob lock may be adequate for the bathroom, but it is wholly unacceptable for the front door. An intruder can simply grasp the knob with a vise grip and twist until the whole assembly tears loose. Have a mortise lock installed with a dead bolt that protrudes at least an inch. Watch out for spring-loaded locks that latch automatically. A thief can slide a credit card around the door to push the bolt back.

A lock that requires a key on both sides (to get in as well as to get out) is sometimes necessary if the door is close to a window, since an intruder might break the glass and release the lock from the inside. Nevertheless, you must take care that you do not inadvertently make your home a firetrap by having doors that lock you in with the flames. A better idea is to board up those ornamental windows around your front door.

Secondary locks. Your doors should have secondary locks as well. Choose a vertical dead bolt lock—one in which several vertically moving dead bolts engage a series of steel loops affixed to the door frame. Such locks cannot be defeated by an intruder who uses a crowbar or automobile jack to push the frame away from the door.

Lock picking. Remember that all but the most sophisticated locks can be picked. An expert can get through most key locks in a matter of minutes, if not seconds. You also should guard against your keys being borrowed and duplicates, or wax impressions, being made of each. Never give a parking attendant your entire key ring. Similarly, be careful about handing your key ring to locker or pool attendants for safekeeping. Never leave a key under the doormat or in any other place close to the door it opens.

Chains. Chains on doors are helpful for seeing who is on the other side, although a peephole is far superior. You should know that a chain will not stop someone for long. They can easily be jimmied, severed with a bolt cutter, or simply snapped (or pulled out of the wall) by someone throwing their weight against the door.

Sliding French doors. Sliding French doors should be fitted with shatterproof glass. Brace bars should be inserted in the door tracks to keep them from being forced open. If you don't have a brace bar, stick a sawed-off broom handle into the track to keep the door from sliding in the event the lock is forced. In addition, place screws in the upper track to prevent the door from being lifted from the bottom track, and add a vertical locking device.

Windows. The most reliable method of protecting windows from intrusion is to cover them with bars or decorative wrought iron. Steel shutters that can be locked from the inside are even better.

At the very least, windows should be drilled with a hole where a nail (or a special locking bolt) can prevent the window from being opened. Remember that an intruder can always shatter the glass to undo a latch, so shatterproof panes installed in a frame that cannot be knocked out are desirable. Do not neglect to secure upstairs windows or balcony doors that can be reached from trees or adjoining buildings.

If your threat level is very high, consider covering your windows with Mylar or some similar window treatment, which makes them impervious to most small arms as well as to the blast effects from bombs or grenades going off in the vicinity. Mylar reduces the light coming through the windows only marginally, and it will not shatter when struck with a sledgehammer (providing the window frame is of equal strength). Be advised, however, that such material is quite expensive.

In some extremely dangerous countries, antigrenade screens are required. These do not have to look like prison bars, although heavy grating certainly will help deter intruders. Many different materials will do the job. Local building materials companies generally sell chain-link screen, which is commonly used on school gymnasiums to prevent objects such as baseballs from breaking windows. Any screening material of this type should stop a hand grenade or Molotov cocktail.

Securing the House

Good lighting. A well-lit house is hard to penetrate. Lights at each corner of your house will provide general coverage. Do not forget lighting beyond the boundaries of your own property. Some security systems don't permanently light the entire property; instead, every light goes on automatically if an intruder trips an infrared beam.

If you have done your homework, you should live in a residential area with good street lighting. If not, anticipate possible avenues of approach to your property and set up lighting to ensure the maximum amount of exposed ground between the intruder's cover and your home.

Alarms. At the very least, all doors and windows on the ground floor should be wired with an alarm system. To be even more secure, all upper-floor windows and doors (leading to sun decks, balconies, and so on) should be included in the system. You also might want to create a second line of defense within the house using motion or infrared detectors or pressure-sensitive mats. The system should have an automatic dial-out capability, whereby the police are alerted whenever an alarm is tripped.

Your alarm system should have a battery or generator backup. Otherwise, the intruder can simply cut the electrical cables leading into your house to incapacitate the system.

Alarms should be installed by a reputable company. To ascertain a company's reputation, check with the local police as well as with the Better Business Bureau and other consumer organizations. Avoid companies with a reputation for installing systems characterized by frequent false alarms. This usually is indicative of inferior systems, inadequate servicing, poor installation, or all three. Remember, just because a system costs a great deal of money does not mean it will work properly. One new owner of a Beverly Hills mansion discovered that the $500,000 alarm system in the house was totally useless because it had been incorrectly installed. The entire system had to be replaced.

In recent years, the home security industry has had a high rate of bankruptcies and business failures. Look for a company that has a good track record and is likely to be around in a year or two when you require servicing. Remember, it may be difficult to get replacement components for off-brand security systems.

Another reason to use a well-established and reputable company is that an employee of the company could use the blueprints of your home and the alarm system to plan his own break-in. No one knows the vulnerabilities of your home better than the people who install your alarm system.

Response force. Your alarm system does not stop an intruder; it simply lets you know that he is there, and some systems let him know that he has been discovered. Having been alerted, you will still have to summon help; (if it is not done automatically), drive off the intruder, flee the scene, or take cover. It is recommended that you have a safe room in your house to retire to until help arrives.

A call to local police is generally the best strategy, although some people enjoy the additional security that comes from retaining a private response force that also can be summoned in such situations. The best alarm systems are usually connected to a central station manned twenty-four hours a day by a security firm, which responds automatically when an alarm goes off.

Evacuation plan. You and your family should have an evacuation plan for your home. The moment a terrorist or kidnapper bursts into your house is no time to start thinking about your response. Figure out various ways to get out of the house quickly if you are threatened and rehearse the procedures with your family. You also should designate a safe rendezvous point where you can regroup.

Safe room. Like all U.S. embassies, homes in high-risk areas often have a secure room, or bunker, into which family members can escape in time of crisis. The room must be specially constructed and should be strong enough to prevent adversaries from breaking into it for at least ten or fifteen minutes, which should be an adequate amount of time for the police or your response force to arrive on the scene.

Since attacks occur most often at night, consider locating the safe room near the master bedroom. The door of the safe room should be steel and have several heavy dead bolt locks. The walls, and if possible the ceiling and floor, should be steel, aluminum, or concrete.

Inside the safe room, keep a supply of food, water, and other emergency supplies such as a flashlight, extra batteries, and bandages and antiseptic. In addition, the room should be outfitted with a fire extinguisher, gas masks (respirators), a telephone, and a two-way radio so that you can call for help. Some safe rooms have panic buttons that notify the police or your security detail of the crisis. A world-band radio also is useful in Third World countries so that you can find out what is going on outside in times of civil strife or revolution.

Firebombs and arson. Do not neglect the threat from arson or firebomb attack. Windows facing the street should be constructed with shatterproof panes or protected by bars and screens. Smoke alarms should be placed in all rooms, particularly in the bedroom area. Fire extinguishers should be placed at strategic points around the house; while the canisters are unsightly, they can be concealed behind drapes or furniture. Make certain family members and household staff know the location of each extinguisher. Fire extinguishers should be of the ABC type, capable of handling wood, grease, or electrical fires. Note that all furnishings made of polyethylene will emit toxic hydrogen cyanide gas during a fire. These should be replaced.

Following Household Safety Procedures

I.D. checks. No one in your household should ever admit anyone without proper identification. Terrorists and thieves can easily obtain bogus police or repairmen's uniforms. Anyone who comes to the door should be checked out thoroughly. Read his or her identification card carefully; don't let the person simply flash it at you. If a repairman or delivery person arrives unexpectedly, check by telephone with his or her place of business to make sure he or she is legitimate. Look up the number yourself before you call, as a number the person gives you could be that of an accomplice.

Remember that U.S. general James Dozier was kidnapped and held prisoner for six weeks by Red Brigades terrorists who gained access to his apartment by impersonating plumbers investigating a leak. In Guatemala, a woman was kidnapped by terrorists who gained admission to her house by dressing as nuns. Don't trust anyone you don't know, even a nun or a priest.

Surveillance. Terrorist surveillance often starts at your home. Take note of any suspicious people wandering about the area, asking about you, or trying to engage you or a member of your household staff in conversation. Watch what you put in your garbage can, as it may be sifted for pieces of intelligence. In this regard, you might want to consider the purchase of a small desktop or floor shredder. The best shredders are those that turn paper into confetti rather than long strips. Remember that Iranian militants who took over the U.S. embassy in Tehran painstakingly reassembled all the classified documents that had been shredded in strips.

Also beware of panel trucks and other vehicles parked on the street in your neighborhood for a long period of time. The truck might have one-way glass and be packed with electronic eavesdropping gear. If you see men working on telephone lines near your house, you may want to double-check with the telephone company to make sure the workers are not imposters tapping your phone line. Pay particular attention to vacant houses or apartments in proximity to your house to make certain that they are not turned into observation posts.

Telephones. Terrorists or kidnappers may tap your telephone, so do not discuss business, personal, or travel plans over the phone. An unlisted telephone number will give you some protection and will keep you from being bothered by phone solicitations. Do not hand your number out indiscriminately and make it a point to take your business calls at your place of business.

Never identify yourself to a caller. Ask for the caller's identity and the name of whomever he or she is trying to reach. Never tell the person your number; ask for the number he or she is trying to reach and if that is not your number, inform them of their mistake and hang up.

Do not be tricked into an ambush by a telephone call. If you receive an emergency call from the police or hospital, inform them that you will call back in one minute, then check the number they give you against the one listed in the telephone book. If you receive a call purportedly from a hospital informing you that your wife or child has been injured, call the hospital to verify that the person in question has been admitted.

Never place a phone on a table in front of a window. All an assassin has to do is telephone your house, and a victim will step into view.

Arrange with your family a system of code words to indicate that there is trouble. An innocuous phrase or a reference to a relative you do not have can be used to indicate that a family member is in trouble or an ambush is waiting for you on your return to the house.

If you have been threatened, attach a recorder to your telephone to record any suspicious calls. If you get threatening calls, contact the local police, your company's security office, and, if abroad, the U.S. consulate. If you are the target of obscene calls, do not argue with the caller, just hang up and contact the police.

Emergency numbers. The numbers of the fire and police departments, ambulance service, and other emergency services should be prominently displayed by the telephone. You also might want to include the phone number of your company's security officer and those of trusted friends, although this may be information that you do not want to fall into the wrong hands.

Eavesdropping devices. Beware of bugs. They are smaller and more sophisticated than ever before. Any transducer (even those that are normally used for broadcasting only, such as those in your stereo or television speakers) can be transformed into a bug. A bug inserted in your telephone handset can record conversations in the room even though the phone is not lifted off the hook.

If the CIA or KGB wants to bug you, they are so technologically sophisticated that you'll probably never find it. Sweeping a house for bugs is extremely costly and time-consuming. Distrust any firm that claims it can do a thorough job in just a few hours. Forget about cheap gadgets that are supposed to tell you if you are being bugged; they can detect only the most rudimentary eavesdropping devices.

Scramblers. The most reliable method of ensuring that your telephone conversations remain private is to purchase a scrambler for every phone on which privacy is desired. This can become expensive, and if there is an eavesdropping device in the room where you use the telephone, your conversation can still be compromised.

A portable scrambler attached to a pay phone or a cellular car phone ensures an extremely secure means of communication. Take care, however, to secure your scrambler phone when you are not using it so that a bug is not placed inside.

Mail. All mail should be handled with extreme care. Plastic explosives (plastique) can be molded into a variety of shapes and forms or rolled out in flat sheets and placed in an envelope. Today's thin batteries and tiny detonators make bombs all the more difficult to detect. Learn how to identify potential bombs (see chapter 8). If you suspect a package or envelope, do not handle it. Clear the room and call the police immediately. Never handle anything left on your doorstep.

In addition to bombs, mail also has been contaminated with poison or other toxic or infectious substances. In the 1970s, toxic material was mailed to several high government officials, including a justice of the Supreme Court.

Mailboxes also can be booby-trapped. In recent years, everything from bombs to rattlesnakes has been left in mailboxes, so use caution when opening your box.

In high-risk areas, you might consider having all your mail, personal and professional, sent to your place of business, where you can establish a screening process by trained individuals.

Special precautions. Do not make it easy for any terrorist or other adversary to observe or snipe at you. At night, avoid flipping on the lights without first drawing the shades; with a light behind you, you are starkly silhouetted and an easy target. Make a habit of leaving on all your lights after dark. Turning lights on and off will permit terrorists to pinpoint which room you are occupying. The Israeli commandos who killed the operational chief of the PLO, Abu Jihad, in early 1988 observed his movements by means of the lights in his house being flicked off and on. They knew he had finally retired for the night when the last light in the house was turned off. It was at that moment that they made their move.

Protecting Your Children

Make certain that your children understand the seriousness of good security procedures and punish them when they fail to observe basic rules. Remember that children are far more trusting than adults and are less likely to question a stranger at the door or a letter or parcel addressed to them. Your children also should be told not to discuss family security arrangements with friends and schoolmates.

School. To reduce the risk of one of your children being kidnapped, especially if you are living abroad, see that they are driven to school. They are easy targets when traveling on foot, standing on a corner waiting for a school bus, or using public transportation.

Remember, children are at the mercy of careless teachers. Instruct your children's teachers never to allow them to depart with anyone but you or your spouse. Keep in touch with teachers, paying particular attention to field trips or outings planned for the class. Anticipate trouble before it happens and make certain that your children stay home when any activity that could leave them vulnerable to assault or kidnapping is planned.

Whistles or horns. Give your children whistles or air horns and instruct them to use these in an emergency. Obviously, no one attracted by the noise can stop a full-scale terrorist assault, but a horn may deter an amateur kidnapper or pervert.

Your children should carry the horns or whistles in their pockets and not on a string around their necks. An assailant could try to grab the horn or whistle and strangle the child in the process.

Training Your Household Staff

One of the more important aspects of your personal safety is your domestic staff. Your maid will normally have access to your keys, may live in your house, and will know your routine. Whether you want to or not, you will be trusting such people with your life.

Screen your staff. Always check the background of each staff member. Contact all references provided; if the person has no references, don't hire him or her. Also check the person's name with the police and, if you have a corporate security department, with your security chief. If you are living abroad, contact the U.S. consulate, which will have its own list of dangerous people. Indeed, the consulate may be able to steer you to people they have already investigated. Contact your friends for names of domestics they have employed and found trustworthy.

Do not underestimate your own ability to spot trouble. You and your spouse should conduct separate interviews of each applicant. If you sense that something is amiss, reject the applicant. Trust your instincts.

Treat your staff generously and with respect. When danger threatens, your maid may save your life; then again, she may not, depending on how you have treated her. Your servants and household staff should be treated with respect. You cannot demand the trust and devotion of your household staff; it must be earned.

Use your staff to provide local intelligence. Local intelligence is vital, and a loyal servant can provide you with lots of it. As noted earlier, any criminal or terrorist operation against you or members of your family is likely to begin with a period of surveillance. Your household staff will be familiar with the routine of your neighborhood and might spot something that looks suspicious or out of place. Describe potential threats to your household staff and instruct them to watch for signs of trouble. Indeed, meet with them on a regular basis regarding such problems and fears. Remind them that they have a personal stake in spotting trouble before it happens, since they also run the risk of becoming victims of a terrorist or criminal assault on the household.

Integrate your staff into your security procedures. The staff should know how to take precautions on the telephone or when answering the door. Make a point of reinforcing household security precautions so that the staff does not grow lax. Make major security breaches or oversights an automatic reason for dismissal.

Have your staff take some routine precautions. Among the routine precautions your staff should take are the following:

- They should never speak with anyone about you, your family, the house, or your security procedures.
- They should not admit anyone to the house without prior clearance from you. (This will require a good deal of foresight on your part.)
- They should admit no one without proper identification. If there is any question about a person's identity, he or she should be required to wait outside until the staff checks with his or her office or employer.
- They should be suspicious of new delivery personnel or utility inspectors, especially if they claim to be substituting for a sick coworker.

Give your staff first aid training. Since your servants probably will spend a great deal of time with your children, you might want to train them in first aid and CPR. In addition, you might want to send them to a rudimentary security awareness course provided by a professional firm.

Choosing an Apartment

Some apartments can be far safer than a house. Apartment managers often conduct an extensive investigation of each prospective tenant. Moreover, many apartment complexes have twenty-four-hour doormen and receptionists, closed-circuit television, and locked underground garages. Some apartment complexes do not provide these services, however, so you should shop around and use common sense.

Special precautions. Choose an apartment above the second floor to reduce the likelihood of an intruder forcing open your windows or balcony doors. At the same time, do not get an apartment so elevated that fire fighters cannot reach you in an emergency. Check with the fire department in your area to see how high its ladders reach.

Be careful in apartment elevators. Never get on with a stranger if you are a threatened person. Indeed, beware of all strangers in the building. Never hold a door open for someone who walks up behind you unless you know him or her. Do not assume that someone lives in the complex simply because the person acts as though he or she belongs there. Some years ago, the Watergate complex in Washington was plagued by a rash of burglaries. When the burglar was finally apprehended, he turned out to be an elderly, distinguished-looking man who habitually wore a natty blue blazer and ascot. He visited the complex so often that residents assumed he was a resident and regularly held the door open for him.

Parking garages. The most dangerous area in any apartment complex is likely to be the parking garage. It should be well lit, preferably patrolled, and accessible only with a key, access card, or remote control device. If possible, try to get a parking place near the door or elevator to the building.

Other tenants. If the other tenants don't take security seriously, you should move to a more security-conscious complex.

Apartment staff. Insist that all maintenance workers, desk workers, doormen, and other apartment personnel are screened before they are hired. In addition, all movers, carpenters and decorators, painters, and repairmen should be required to sign in and out and wear identification badges while in the apartment building.

6

Business Security

AMERICAN business abroad is no longer protected by the supremacy of the United States in world affairs. During the so-called American Century, which in reality lasted a little more than sixty years, the United States made and enforced most of the rules governing international commerce. It was rarely reluctant to punish or overthrow an errant banana republic making noises about nationalizing U.S. interests or to threaten intervention in a foreign land to secure the release of a hostage businessman. One need only recall Secretary of State John Hay's ringing demand for "Perdicaris alive or Raisuli dead" to realize the lengths to which the U.S. government would once go to save an American businessman from the clutches of a foreign terrorist.

Today the United States no longer enjoys the supremacy in world affairs it once did. It is challenged economically by a revitalized Europe and Japan and militarily by the Soviet Union. Moreover, many Third World countries employ terrorists and other proxy forces to conduct vicious and often deniable attacks against American targets.

The eclipse of U.S. military might and influence during the past two decades has meant that American business finds itself with enormous assets abroad at a time when U.S. power is in decline. Confronted with the rising wave of violence against American targets, the U.S. government has, for the most part, been characterized by vacillation and timidity in recent years.

You can no longer rely on the U.S. government for protection abroad, no matter how egregious the threat from a foreign government or terrorist organization.

Multinational corporations have no choice but to accommodate to this change. Added to this is the failure of federal, state, and local governments to deal effectively with the issue of crime and violence at home. As a result, corporate security outlays have been rising consistently for decades, and it is reliably reported that by 1990 1 percent of the U.S. gross national product (GNP) will be devoted to home and industrial security. This trend disturbs most top corporate managers, who regard security costs as nonproductive expenditures. It also means that every security dollar must be spent as carefully as possible. While good security clearly makes good sense, corporate security programs too often are poorly conceived and executed, characterized by redundancies and waste, and not properly integrated into the company's overall stategic planning.

Today, no senior corporate manager can afford not to be concerned and informed about security matters and how his or her company's security dollars are spent. Security is not something that can simply be delegated to others.

Corporate Intelligence

The difference between success and failure often is information. We live in the information age, and any company that ignores this fact does so at its own peril. According to one recent survey, 80 percent of the Fortune 500 companies surveyed increased their corporate intelligence budgets in the last three years.

Counterintelligence operations. Don't live in a fool's paradise. Assume that your company is an intelligence target of your competitors and possibly even the media. If your company is engaged in high-tech research or defense production, it may even be a target of foreign intelligence services.

Protect yourself and your corporate assets not only with effective security procedures, but also by establishing a corporate counterintelligence capability. Don't wait for industrial espionage to come to your attention; aggressively try to ferret it out.

Risk assessment. Multinational companies require of the international system, if not stability, then at least predictability. There is no such thing as a risk-free foreign environment for doing business. Thus, your goal must be to manage risk, or as General George Patton once said, "Take calculated risks. That is quite different from being rash."

If you operate abroad, your company should establish a country risk management group to monitor political and economic change, instability and violence, and other trends and indicators. This will give you the ability to measure international political risk and factor it into your strategic planning process.

If you lack an in-house capability, consider hiring outside consultants to redress this information deficiency. Companies such as Miami-based Ackerman & Palumbo, London's Control Risks Ltd., and Risks International of a Washington, D.C., suburb attempt to keep tabs on terrorist violence and general economic, social, and political conditions throughout the world.

Country risk. As an essential element of environmental forecasting, you should seek answers to questions such as the following:

- How stable is the host country's political system?
- How long is the host government likely to remain in power?
- Is there active political violence in the country? At whom is it directed? What groups are involved? Do they receive outside help? What is their history of targets and operations?

- How closely is the United States related with the host government?
- What effect would a violent change of government have on the business climate?

Vulnerabilities

Threats to your company can take many forms. Kidnappings and bombs occupy center stage, but potential threats to your company are as unlimited as the human imagination.

Inventory control. Pilferage and theft represent a major problem for virtually every company in the United States.

Hoaxes and threats. Half of all terrorist incidents are hoaxes. Yet if they are taken seriously (which is the only prudent course of action), they can be very disruptive and have a negative impact on your company, its profits, and the morale of your employees.

Sabotage. Production lines and corporate operations can be sabotaged in many ways. Abrasives such as sand can be added to fuel or thrown into moving parts. Gumming agents, such as sugar in the gas tank, can be employed. Wrenches can be thrown into machinery, and objects can be loosened so that vibrations will cause them to fall into moving parts. A saboteur can tamper with gauges or render warning devices inoperative. "Viruses" can be introduced into your company's computers to trigger system shutdowns, rearrange or destroy files, or ignore critical warnings or other information.

Industrial espionage. Both competitors and foreign agents can steal corporate secrets. This is a particularly difficult crime to counter since nothing is physically taken and there is rarely any evidence of the loss.

Arson. Fire is a constant threat to most firms engaged in manufacturing. The storage of fuel, dangerous chemicals, and other combustibles will make the arsonist's job easier. Consider what the loss of your company's files or computers would mean to its future.

Attacks on employees. Terrorists and criminals may carry out attacks on your employees, who have a right, within reason, to a secure workplace and to protection elsewhere from attacks motivated solely by their relationship to the company.

Product tampering can be devastating to corporate profits. The 1982 Tylenol poisonings, although well handled by the company and its chairman, resulted in a $500 million loss of profits.

Security Guards

Hire people who take their jobs seriously. Generally, you get what you pay for. A minimum-wage, poorly trained, and unmotivated security guard force is unlikely to perform particularly well on a day-to-day basis, much less during a crisis. In addition, such a force probably will be characterized by absenteeism, sloppy work, and a lack of pride and discipline.

Checking security badges, watching television monitors, scanning bags in an x-ray machine, and patrolling the premises all require concentration and attention to detail. Much of the work is boring, and a guard who waves employees through a checkpoint in a perfunctory manner without closely scrutinizing their I.D. cards is not performing his job properly. Horror stories abound. So lax were security standards at TRW, a leading defense contractor, that convicted Soviet spy Christopher J. Boyce recounted the story of how his immediate supervisor had pasted a chimpanzee's face on his security badge and regularly passed through security checkpoints. In another instance, an employee of the federal government taped a photograph of Libyan strongman Muammar Qaddafi over his I.D. On the sign-in sheet under "affiliation," he wrote that he was a member of the Islamic Jihad. The guard paid no attention and waved him through.

Require security personnel to be tactful and polite. To perform their jobs effectively, your security staff will need the cooperation of the rest of your employees. A guard or supervisor who abuses his or her power will create friction, causing resentment against the very precautions that exist for the protection of the company and its employees.

Inform your employees why various security precautions have been taken. In this way, security precautions will seem less arbitrary. Employees who understand and share your concern regarding the elements of good security can be expected to be more security conscious and cooperative.

Make certain that your security guards have received sufficient training. They should be able to handle routine problems in a courteous and professional manner. A well-trained guard is less likely to overreact in a stressful situation.

If guards are issued any kind of weapon (including a baton or nightstick but especially a gun), be sure that they know how to use it and are in full compliance with local laws. Use of a weapon should be delineated by specific rules of engagement devised by management, your legal counsel, and your security chief. Remember, a security guard not trained in unarmed combat is far more likely to use his gun if he perceives a threatening situation.

Security personnel should be trained to take the initiative in a crisis. They should be familiar with all major corporate vulnerabilities and receive periodic threat assessments so that they will know what to expect. A good security guard also should know the elements of first aid and fire-fighting procedures.

The enemies of good security are routine and boredom. A mechanical, repetitious schedule dulls the senses of your security personnel and leads to inattentiveness. Left for long periods of time at isolated posts, your security personnel will lose their edge and become vulnerable to surprise attacks.

To the extent possible, vary their routines and assignments. Hold frequent drills. In fact, the more drills held, the better, since these will not only hone the skills of your security personnel but enhance their morale as well. Indeed, you should constantly test the alertness and reactions of your security guards. Have people unknown to your guards attempt to sneak into your plant or corporate headquarters or try to pass through security checkpoints with forged I.D. cards and various excuses. Park a suspicious vehicle near the building to see how long it takes your guard force to notice it and respond appropriately. See if infiltrators can get access to classified document storage areas or critical machinery.

Make your security personnel feel that their jobs are important. There is a tendency to regard security personnel in the same way you regard the fire extinguisher tucked away behind a glass door—important only in an emergency. Instead, security personnel should be made to feel that they are part of the corporate family, a critical element in the production of the product or service you sell, and no less important than the engineering, marketing, or legal staff.

Whatever you do, don't treat a security guard like a bag carrier or an extra set of hands who can be assigned to any mundane job around the company. If you treat guards as anything less than professionals, they will probably behave in less than a professional manner when an emergency arises.

Solicit the opinions of your security staff on a regular basis. No one should know better whether there are any chinks in your corporate defenses.

Don't expose your guards to unnecessary risks. A hardened guard booth and closed-circuit television will make your guards less vulnerable and better able to respond in the event of a surprise attack or other emergency. Moreover, guards posted outside at the gate or at strategic locations around the complex will be more alert and effective if they are not forced to stand unprotected to the elements. A guard standing in a downpour or in the tropical sun for hours on end is more likely to be concerned with his own discomfort than with checking I.D. cards and scrutinizing vehicles.

Perimeter Security

Fences. Don't wait until the threat is inside your building before addressing it. Your facility should be surrounded by a double fence that will intercept threats before they reach you and your headquarters or plant. Fences define what is yours and permit your guards to control access to the high-consequence targets on your property.

Fences should be embedded in concrete. You also might want to top them off with barbed or concertina wire, but remember that a determined intruder can throw a blanket over such wire or wear heavy clothes to protect himself.

Combine fences with sensors. Sensors (infrared, motion, and so on) will tell you when someone has penetrated your perimeter and should permit you to respond to the specific location. When you are choosing and installing sensors, reliability should be your overriding goal. A sensor system that produces too many false alarms breeds indifference in your guard force. Also consider having closed-circuit television cameras placed at critical points along your fences.

Your fences should act as "beaten zones." They should form part of a belt of bare ground that extends completely around a particular site, in this case your property. An intruder must cross this area without the benefit of any cover. Bearing this in mind, place all fences away from buildings or other obstructions to your guard's line of sight.

Remember that a barrier without a response force is no real deterrent. Fences and walls do not stop an intruder; they merely slow him up and make him vulnerable to detection. Thus, if at all possible, you should maintain some kind of response force to patrol the fences and respond to intrusions.

A tall chain-link fence may stop grenades and even rockets fired in your direction, but a fence is no substitute for hardening your buildings. A rocket-propelled grenade detonating in a tall fence will still scatter shrapnel over a wide area.

Consider creating an in-depth defense. Within your perimeter, set up additional zones of defense around high-value targets such as your computer center, warehouses containing flammable material, and corporate headquarters.

Consider creating security access roads. If your facility is a large estate or plantation, consider creating roads running around the perimeter for your security vehicles. If possible, the roads should be hard surfaced and thereby passable under all weather conditions, since guerrillas may take advantage of inclement weather to mask their attack. Cut back brush and trees on both sides of the road to reduce the risk of an ambush.

Minimize gaps in your defense. The fewer the entrances, the more your security force can be concentrated in certain areas. Intruders can easily rush a gate manned by a single guard or slip through while he is distracted. Eliminate unnecessary points of entrance/exit and concentrate your manpower on the remaining points.

Provide some means of preventing individuals from sneaking in behind or clinging underneath authorized vehicles. All vehicle entrances should be within sight of a guardhouse or monitored by a closed-circuit camera. Even better, guards should be posted at the entrance to inspect each vehicle that comes and goes. A mirror mounted on the end of a long pole is handy for looking under vehicles for bombs or unwanted passengers.

Mark your fences. Depending on the laws of your host country, you could be held liable for any injury caused by your barricades and fences. Barbed-wire or concertina fences should be easy to see, but you might want to hang strips of brightly colored cloth on them to increase their visibility. Electrified fences should be clearly marked as such, with signs posted at frequent intervals.

Lighting

Unless your guards have special night vision equipment, they will depend primarily on their sight to spot intruders. The cleared zone formed by your double fence should be illuminated by floodlights, leaving no shadows where an intruder could hide. Provide extra lighting around your guard stations to keep an assailant from sneaking up on them. Provide enough lighting at checkpoints so that your guards can see what they are doing, but don't overlight an area and make it so bright that it impairs the night vision of those working there.

Don't allow your guards to be silhouetted so that a sniper can see them. Your guards should be able to see without being seen. Angle your lighting outward so that it is directed at an intruder, perhaps even making it difficult for him to see what is going on inside your compound. In this way, your guards will remain cloaked in shadows.

Enhance the effect of your lights by painting buildings and walls a light color. If you do this, an intruder wearing dark clothing will stand out much more easily. Light-colored surroundings also reflect back much of the light that hits them, in effect increasing the power of your lamps. Dark surroundings absorb light and require much stronger lamps to obtain the same level of lighting you can achieve with light-colored buildings.

Summary. Your guards will detect intruders by their movements and the contrast they pose to their backgrounds. Broad, cleared zones around your facility, well-placed lighting, and a light background are all critical to good security.

Alarms and Locks

There are a variety of alarms on the market. The various salesmen will undoubtedly tell you the advantages of each, so I will concentrate on the shortcomings.

Alarms passing a current through a wire or strip of metallic foil. When a window or door protected in this fashion is opened, the wire or foil contact is broken, interrupting the current and triggering the alarm. Although this type of alarm is simple and cheap, an intruder often can bridge the current using his own wire. Alternatively, he can go around the system, perhaps cutting his way through plasterboard walls. Such a system will inform your security personnel that someone attempted to get inside or actually did get inside, but it will not help locate the intruder.

Other systems use an infrared beam of light which, when broken, sounds the alert. This type of system is reliable and easily employed to cover areas that cannot be sealed by doors or walls. It may even be of some use in detecting fires, although this capability should not be overstated since the beams are often set near the ground, not close to the ceiling where smoke gathers.

Be aware that dust or steam can sometimes trigger infrared alarms. Moreover, when they are used outside, rain, leaves, swaying shrubs, and animals may trigger them.

Ultrasonic or microwave alarms. An ultrasonic or microwave alarm broadcasts its signal into the room, then listens to the pattern of returning echoes. Any motion in the room will distort the pattern and sound the alarm. Such alarms usually identify the presence of an intruder, but somone moving very slowly or staying beneath tables and chairs may be able to sneak by the alarm. In addition, certain materials absorb sound, and if these materials are present in a sufficient quantity at your facility, they may preclude the use of the system altogether. Finally, air currents caused by air-conditioning or heating ducts will have to be minimized to prevent false alarms.

Other alarms detect sounds using microphones. With this type of alarm, you can tap into the microphone to hear what is triggering the alarm. Alarms of this ilk are easily triggered by vibrations and noise from the street or planes passing overhead, so their use is generally limited to secluded buildings or the deeper recesses of a facility. Frequent false alarms may cause your security people to turn down the sensitivity, allowing a real intruder to get by the alarm.

Also, be careful that you do not end up bugging yourself. Any microphone that you plant in your office may be hooked into a bugging system. Your own security people will be able to eavesdrop on your conversations in rooms protected by such systems.

Electromagnetic alarms. An electromagnetic alarm creates an electronic field around any nongrounded metallic object and will sound a warning if that field is disturbed. This type of alarm may offer the fewest disadvantages of any of the alarms mentioned.

Power backup. As with any other sensitive equipment, be sure to provide your alarm system with a backup power source to prevent your defenses from being neutralized by an adversary who cuts your power lines. Indeed, be sure to build redundancies into your security systems and procedures to the extent possible.

Installing and maintaining your alarms. The alarm business in the United States is characterized by a high rate of turnover and failure. In addition, a great deal of alarm equipment is overpriced and poorly designed and manufactured. Thus, let the buyer beware. Check out the history of the companies you are considering. How long have they been in business? Will they provide you with references of satisfied customers? Will they sell you the best equipment on the market or only that equipment for which they have a distributorship? Is each system they design tailored to your specific needs, or do they essentially repeat the same system each time they receive a contract?

At the very least, get multiple bids from a variety of companies and make certain that you understand each proposed system, especially its advantages and disadvantages, so that you can make an informed judgment. Remember that the cheapest system is not necessarily the best system or the most cost-effective over the long run. Guard against companies that offer the system at an artificially low price, then sock it to you in terms of maintenance and other related costs. Generally, your goal should be to choose the most effective, most efficient system.

Precautions preventing an intruder from interfering with the cables from your alarms to the guard station. Your security consultant can recommend several possible ways to prevent this problem. Devices can be installed to detect the drop, or surge, in current caused by an intruder splicing a bypass onto the cables. Alternatively, you might install electrical foil wired to an alarm system around any exposed wiring. The best method is burying the wires or encasing them so that they cannot be reached at all.

Keys. While all key-operated locks can be picked, do not make the intruder's task any easier. Keep a strict accounting of all keys, particularly duplicates, which should be kept and regularly inventoried by your security office. Skeleton keys, or master keys that open a variety of locks, should be carefully guarded and never identified (keys marked "master key" might as well have a "steal me" sign attached to them). Remember that all locks configured for master keys are easier to pick than others, so forgo some convenience and buy the type of lock that has no master key.

Opt for a flexible, rather than a rigid, system. You may have to alter the configuration of your system on a regular basis. The most frequent reason is to make certain that a former employee no longer has access to company files. Thus, buy locks with removable plugs that can be changed as needed. In addition, most ultrasonic, electromagnetic, or photovoltaic alarms can be purchased in modular units that can be moved and installed as required.

Employees

Screen all employees, even top management. A top headhunting firm in New York recently found that more than 50 percent of the executive résumés it surveyed were substantially inflated. Some contained outright lies. Thus, it is a wise policy to run background checks on all potential employees to ascertain whether key information contained on their résumés is accurate. It also is useful to learn whether potential employees have drug, alcohol, or similar problems because such things clearly affect job performance.

In foreign countries, it is even more important that you know whom you are hiring, including clerical and janitorial help. Known terrorists have infiltrated a number of multinational firms before carrying out attacks.

Consider administering polygraphs. Although polygraphs are highly controversial in some quarters, this author is a strong advocate of administering polygraph tests to all employees on a regular basis. While no employee should be fired solely on the basis of a polygraph test, it may alert you to a problem that can be verified by other means. In addition, the knowledge that polygraph tests are administered to all employees often serves as a deterrent to would-be thieves, industrial spies, and terrorists who might be considering infiltrating your company or organization.

Be particularly cautious about temporary help. Since it is generally impossible to screen temporary employees, make certain that they are carefully monitored by both their supervisors and your security staff. Their I.D. badges should be different from those of regular employees, and these badges should restrict them from entering sensitive areas of the company.

Similarly, outside contractors and their personnel should be provided with I.D. badges that clearly identify them as such. They should be escorted and monitored by your security staff whenever they are working in or near sensitive areas. They should never be given free run of your facility.

Educate your employees about the elements of good security. Explain that the security measures you have adopted are for their own protection and the well-being of the company. Enlist their assistance in reporting strange or suspicious behavior on the part of other employees. Many of U.S. Navy radioman Jerry Whitworth's fellow workers were suspicious of his affluence, which was inconsistent with his rank and salary, but no one raised the issue with his superiors. For years, Whitworth, a member of the infamous Walker spy ring, passed material to John Walker for sale to the Soviets.

Terminate employees who violate security procedures. Anyone who routinely disregards your company's security procedures should be terminated. If an employee who sets a bad example is allowed to go unpunished, he or she is likely to encourage similar behavior on the part of others.

Internal Security

Locked files. Don't make it easy for someone to learn your business secrets. Store all files in fireproof cabinets with combination locks. Consider creating an internal classification system that restricts certain classes of information to specific individuals who have been thoroughly investigated.

Clean desk policy. As in some government agencies, require that desks be cleared at the end of each workday. This ensures that no sensitive documents will be left out for anyone, including the cleaning crew, to see.

Computers. Adopt good computer security procedures that prevent unauthorized employees from obtaining access to sensitive files without using the proper access code. Secure all floppy disks at night and lock them in a safe, fireproof place.

7

Executive Protection

An increasing number of prominent and wealthy people and their families are threatened by terrorists, kidnappers, disgruntled employees, and kooks. As a result, the demand for executive protection specialists has never been greater. This is a relatively new phenomenon, however. As E.J. Criscuoli, executive vice president of the American Society for Industrial Security (ASIS), has observed, executive protection used to be "something we never worried about." When Criscuoli got into the security business in the mid-1950s, "as far as most security personnel were concerned, the only person who got executive protection was the President of the United States. Well, there are some corporations today . . . that provide executive protection for their chief executive officer [CEO] that ranks on a par with what is provided to the President of the United States." It is a simple matter of economics, says Criscuoli: If anything happens to the CEO, it might have a negative effect on the company's performance and the value of its stock. He views executive protection as a kind of insurance policy.

Today's threat environment demands more than what one observer called "big Samoans with small minds and large bulges in their coat pockets." Nothing less than skilled protection professionals will suffice. The following suggestions are designed to assist you in selecting and administering your protection detail, working with your bodyguards on a day-to-day basis, and evaluating their performance.

Selecting Your Bodyguards

You don't want Dirty Harry as a bodyguard. The bodyguard's job is the avoidance of threats, so bodyguards should be chosen for the size of their brains, not the width of their shoulders. Bodyguards who view their role primarily as one of shooting it out with the adversary are to be avoided at all costs. Reflecting this emphasis on professionalism and mastered skills, women are becoming bodyguards in increasing numbers and are doing well at the job.

If your bodyguards rely on their firepower and muscles to ensure your safety, at the expense of good security practices, you are in trouble. Good security is first and foremost an intellectual activity requiring judgment and training. A carload of bodyguards will usually not save you if you are drawn into a trap because of carelessness or stupidity on the part of your security detachment. When Aldo Moro, the leader of Italy's Christian Democrats, was abducted, the guards riding with him and in an accompanying car were shot to death by the terrorists. One security man managed to roll out of the trailing car and fire back, only to be dispatched by a sniper posted by the terrorists on a nearby roof. Similarly, in the case of German industrialist Hans Martin Schleyer, bodyguards riding with him and behind in a second car were gunned down before they could return fire. Ask any Vietnam combat veteran, and he will tell you that ambushes tend to be bloody, one-sided, and short.

In the final analysis, you want bodyguards who regard their chief responsibility as avoiding trouble but are capable of responding skillfully in the event of an emergency.

More does not always mean better. Some executives insist upon surrounding themselves with a menagerie of thick-necked thugs who may be of some use in blocking bullets but little else. Rely on a few good people who can think on their feet and have impressed you with their common sense.

Low profile. The best security is usually very low-key and not readily evident, although there may be some occasions where a show of force or demonstrable security precautions are a deterrent. If your security detail is composed of only one or two people, they should not be at your side constantly because an assailant will be able to identify who they are. Indeed, the assailant will likely shoot them first and then come after you.

Experience. Your bodyguards should have professional training and experience. Don't just hand a gun to someone and make him a bodyguard, as is often done in Third World countries. Generally, the best American bodyguards are ex–Secret Service agents, former members of Delta Force and SEAL Team Six, and law enforcement officers with practical dignitary protection experience. In addition, a number of private academies turn out competent and capable bodyguards, although you should beware of graduates of fly-by-night schools and inferior training programs.

Remember that the Secret Service is a very large organization, with employees performing many different jobs. Not every member of the Secret Service will have the same skills or experience. Similarly, many corporate executives believe that any member of the FBI or CIA is qualified to serve as a bodyguard. Most FBI agents spend their time apprehending criminals, and most CIA employees are engaged in the collection and analysis of intelligence, so only few individuals in either organization are executive protection specialists.

Police and law enforcement experience does not necessarily mean that an individual is qualified to be a bodyguard. Many former police officers make excellent bodyguards, but additional training is usually required.

Don't be afraid to grill applicants for your security detail about their specific life experiences. Remember that most people, even those in the FBI or Secret Service, have never been in a truly tough situation or faced a real threat. If you are a threatened individual, you want bodyguards who have been tested in real life. By the same token, beware of con artists and those who are long on bluff and bluster but short on specifics. Someone who tells too many war stories may be trying too hard to impress you. Verify to the extent possible the combat record, professional experience, and any alleged awards or combat medals of all protective detail applicants. Beware of anyone who says his background is classified; even those who have held sensitive government positions can verify their employment and activities.

Self-starters. When selecting bodyguards, concentrate on individuals who can anticipate problems before they arise with a minimal amount of guidance and prompting. You cannot do your bodyguard's thinking for him. You will often be distracted or involved in other things, hence your bodyguards will be the only ones concentrating on your security around the clock.

Communication skills and discretion. Every time you go somewhere, your guard will make advance security arrangements. Thus, he will need good communications skills, both written and oral.

He will be your representative, and hence his behavior will reflect on you and your company. Insist on discretion and professionalism. Being on a VIP's protection detail can swell an individual's head. You do not want a guard who precedes you with blustering and pushiness. His arrogance may create hard feelings that will be directed against you. Select guards who can operate quietly and efficiently without making waves.

Also find a bodyguard who can maintain his cool. A nervous bodyguard will drive you crazy.

Education, appearance, and foreign language skills. Education is important for a bodyguard, especially since it will enable him to blend into your world. In this connection, your security detail should be at ease when attending social functions with you or patronizing fine hotels and restaurants. Some executive protection programs include courses on manners, clothing selection, travel, and dining. Your bodyguards generally should wear the same kind of clothing you do (formal, business, casual, and so on). If you are at a black-tie dinner, your guards also should be in black tie. Flashy or colorful clothing should be discouraged, with dark, well-tailored business suits the everyday norm.

If you travel abroad a great deal, it is extremely helpful if one or more members of your security detail can speak a foreign language. Not only will fluency in other languages be useful in making normal arrangements and communicating with local authorities, but it will assist them in spotting trouble and reacting to threats.

Self-discipline. Pay careful attention to your bodyguards' self-discipline. Guard duty is often boring, and guards can become slack. The moment your bodyguard leaves his post to make a personal call or get a drink of water may be the moment the terrorist has been waiting for.

Physical conditioning. Your bodyguards need not be muscle-bound, but physical conditioning is extremely important, especially if you engage in rigorous physical exercise, such as jogging. You don't need bodyguards who can't keep up with you. Similarly, they need to be able to keep up with the pace of your life, which may include long hours and frequent travel. Your bodyguards will often be up long after you are asleep and ready for action before you open your eyes in the morning. A bodyguard not in peak physical shape might not be able to react properly in a crisis.

Around-the-clock protection. Remember, around-the-clock protection ideally requires three eight-hour shifts. If you decide to have only two twelve-hour shifts, you might place too much pressure on your bodyguards and significantly reduce their effectiveness. Nevertheless, three shifts is an expensive proposition, and you must weigh the advantages against the expense.

Medical training. The members of your executive protection detail should be trained in basic first aid and CPR. They should be able to react properly to any medical emergency and know immediately whom to call for additional assistance. Provide your security detail with complete medical information about you and your family, including medical history, drugs and medication you are taking, allergic reactions to any medication, vaccination record, prescription for corrective lenses, and the names, specialties, and phone numbers of all personal physicians.

Guns and other weapons. Executive protection specialists should be weapons qualified and skilled at hand-to-hand combat, but beware of potential bodyguards who place too much emphasis on weapons skills. If you are lucky and your security detail does its job properly, firearms will never be needed. Thus, weapons skills should rank rather low on the list of qualifications for your security detail. Disregard people who run ads such as "Exmerc seeks short-term dangerous assignment. Familiar with knives, automatic weapons, and explosives."

If your security detail is armed, make certain that the guards know how to use their weapons. A jittery guard with a weapon can be a disaster waiting to happen and may harm either you or an innocent bystander. Guards should never draw their weapons unless they intend to use them, and they should be required to pass a skills test on a regular basis. Set down precise rules of engagement governing the use of firearms, such as the threat must be perceived to be life threatening and firearms should be used only as a last resort. Your security detail should be able to deal with most threats without using firearms.

Beware of "cowboys" with weapons that are unsuitable for executive protection, including high-powered pistols such as the .44 magnum, which fires a round that could pass through several walls and unintentionally kill or injure you or a member of your family.

If your protection detail is armed, make certain that they are in compliance with all local and federal laws and regulations. You also might consider purchasing insurance covering accidental death or injury to a member of your security detail or to an innocent bystander stemming from the use of a firearm.

Security training schools. Beware of the training provided by many security schools. While a few have excellent reputations and turn out qualified, competent graduates, others are long on mystique and short on substance. To make an informed judgment, inquire about the backgrounds of the instructors, placement of the school's graduates, and companies and government agencies that have sent employees to the security school.

Keep in mind that a one- or two-week course will not make a chauffeur or a bodyguard an expert. Indeed, a little training might be more dangerous than no training at all, since it might breed a false sense of security.

Working with Your Bodyguards

The cardinal rule is to listen to what your bodyguards have to say. They are your personal security consultants, given the task of overseeing your day-to-day security needs and requirements.

As a business executive, you no doubt are accustomed to taking charge, making decisions, and going where you want and when you want without consulting others. It's your bodyguards' job to advise you, from a security point of view, on your daily routine and activities. If you don't listen to your bodyguards, why have them?

Security requirements are often confining and may take some time to adjust to. One of President Kennedy's former bodyguards said that the president used to pace the floor of the Oval Office at night "like a caged animal" because he could not go anywhere without its becoming a major production. Expect to have problems adjusting, at least initially, to your security program. Over time, your security precautions will likely become second nature and will fit in with your particular lifestyle and needs.

Loss of privacy. Having bodyguards is a very intimate experience, and you will lose some of your privacy. Moreover, if your security team is doing its job properly, members will no doubt ask you many potentially embarrassing questions about your personal life. If you fail to tell your security detail that you have a mistress or are a member of a sex club, you may disrupt their security plans and jeopardize your overall security. Remember, your security is only as good as the weakest link. If kidnappers or terrorists are keeping you under surveillance and learn that you do not take your bodyguards to the hotel where you meet your mistress, they are likely to choose that moment to strike at you.

While portal-to-portal protection is what one often sees in the movies, such protection may be inadequate in many threat environments. If your guard insists that he must stay with you at all times, he is doing so for a reason, and you should heed the advice. This may even mean that he accompanies you to public rest rooms.

Threat analysis. Your security detail will need to spend a good deal of time researching your threat environment so that the guards can plan the best possible defense. All threats against you and your family will have to be taken seriously and carefully analyzed. If you are threatened by terrorists, information will have to be assembled on who they are and on their motivations, methods of attack, weapons, and previous operations. In this way, the threat to you and your family can be placed in perspective, and intelligent decisions regarding your security can be made and implemented.

Advance planning. Ninety percent of executive protection work is advance planning. Not only will your bodyguards constantly collect and analyze intelligence data, but they will map out your movements in advance and make logistical and other preparations, such as hiring suitable vehicles and identifying the nearest hospitals. All such arrangements are vital to your safety, and without them, the rest of your security program is useless.

You can assist your bodyguards in making arrangements by not requiring them to be mind readers. Provide them with your schedule well in advance and try not to make last-minute changes.

Removal from danger. A bodyguard's chief responsibility is to protect you from danger, and in the event that some threat should arise, he should endeavor to remove you from danger as rapidly as possible. If you are confronted by assailants, the bodyguard should position himself between you and the danger and then quickly remove you from the scene. Disabling the attackers is a secondary concern. Indeed, if someone is shooting at you, the bodyguard should push you to the ground or the nearest cover and shield you with his body. Only when you are behind cover should he attempt to shoot back.

There is no shame in running away. Your adversaries may be better armed and have the advantage of surprise. Your goal should be to get away from the scene by whatever means possible.

More experienced bodyguards might have saved the life of Egyptian president Anwar Sadat. They first permitted themselves to be separated from him by officials eager to be photographed near him. When the shooting started, the guards took cover and returned fire instead of protecting Sadat. What cover their leader got was from a few chairs that were thrown over him. U.S. Secret Service agents, regarded as among the best-trained bodyguards in the business, are conditioned to fire back from a standing (not even a crouching) position, absorbing hostile gunfire with their own bodies if necessary.

Your bodyguards should exercise exceptional self-control, particularly if you are subject to heckling or verbal abuse. They should have the presence of mind to move you away from the trouble and the willpower to refrain from hitting or manhandling the heckler. Remember, unnecessary roughness by your bodyguards may result in your being sued.

Help after an attack. Your protective detail should know where the nearest hospital is located and the shortest distance to it in the event you or a member of your family is injured in an attack. After President Reagan was wounded by a would-be assassin, he was rushed to the nearest hospital. At the time, he felt a pain in his chest but believed he had only been bruised. Had the Secret Service agents hesitated, Reagan might not have survived the attack.

You should have a crisis management plan to follow in the event of an emergency. It will indicate who is to be contacted, who is in charge, who is to speak to the media, steps to be taken to prevent attacks on other family members, the disposition of your protective detail at the hospital, and so on. It should be noted that when Reagan was shot, he was temporarily separated from the military aide who was carrying the "football" with the codes for launching the nation's nuclear missiles. The aide had to make his way to George Washington University Hospital by himself but was barred from entry by Secret Service agents who did not know him or his function. It wasn't until he found someone who recognized him that he was able to rejoin the president. While this type of problem had obviously been overlooked, steps were subsequently taken to ensure that it would not happen again. Another example of the poor crisis management procedures in place at the time of Reagan's shooting involved Secretary of State Alexander Haig's misspeaking from the White House that he was "in charge" of the government.

Evaluating your bodyguards. Observe your bodyguards and notice how they react to startling noises and sudden movements. If a guard responds to a disturbance by looking in its direction, he probably needs more training. A bodyguard's first impulse should be to push you to cover, not gawk at a potential threat. If he has to see the threat and size it up before reacting, he may get you killed. He should be programmed to react instinctively, without thinking.

Quality bodyguard training programs often videotape students as they walk through various scenarios to see which way they look and how they react to noises and potential threats. You may want to inquire whether your bodyguards received such training.

In addition, you should make sure that your bodyguards are not easily distracted. At shows, sporting events, and other public appearances, if you are accompanied by only one bodyguard, he should be watching your blind side for any threat attempting to slip up on you. If you have a detail composed of several individuals, each should be assigned a different sector and should never take his eyes off it. Too often, dignitaries are accompanied by bodyguards who, awed by his or her presence, watch the dignitary rather than the crowd.

Respect. Don't treat your bodyguards like errand boys or bag carriers. If you expect them to act like professionals, show them respect. Never ask them to perform tasks that are illegal, such as purchasing drugs for you, or demeaning, such as procuring prostitutes for you. Treat them as though your life may one day depend on them.

Surveillance. Your bodyguards should constantly be alert for signs that you and your security procedures are under surveillance. When you are traveling on foot, one member of your protective detail may want to drop back from time to time to make certain you are not being followed. When not engaged in more pressing business, members of your detail should use their radios to scan other frequencies to see if anyone is talking about you or communicating in a suspicious fashion. They should do the same with a CB radio if one is available.

Communication. Your protective detail should stay in constant touch with either a command post or your security office. When you are traveling and not at a prearranged location, a member of the detail should always remain in touch with your command post or office and the local police in the country you are visiting. Standard equipment includes walkie-talkies and some sort of beeper or paging system to summon reinforcements or indicate a problem. Portable scramblers can be strapped on any telephone and used to communicate privately with your command center or with anyone who has a corresponding scrambler system.

Security etiquette. Good manners should not dictate who precedes whom through a door. Your guard should go first to see what is ahead.

Traveling by car. Attacks on vehicles often take place on the driver's side, as the assailant will first want to incapacitate the driver to stop the vehicle. Your security detail should be alert to attacks from that direction.

Your driver may be a member of your security detail, but at the very least he should be trained in evasive and aggressive driving maneuvers. The driver should be required to rehearse those maneuvers frequently under simulated attack conditions so that when an actual incident occurs, he will not freeze or fail to react properly.

If you have a follow car with additional security guards, that vehicle should always try to interpose itself between your car and any threat. If you run into an ambush where the road is blocked and snipers are deployed on either side, the follow car should swing off the road and allow your car to back out. At the same time, it should be laying down a barrage of fire to cover your retreat.

Once you reach your destination, a member of your protective detail should get out of the car first to survey the area. Only when he is satisfied that everything is in order should he move to your door to open it, shielding you with his body as he does so.

Discretion. Your bodyguards should keep a low profile and always remain discreet, especially around your friends and business associates. The public is fascinated with guns and the cloak-and-dagger nature of security work. Your protective detail should not invite questions. They should never discuss their work for you or your specific security arrangements, and they should not volunteer comments about their profession. Their role is to be seen, not heard. They are not guests at your social or business gatherings; rather, they are present solely to look after your security needs. They should not publicize their work for you or attempt to solicit business contacts at your meetings and social occasions.

Beware of security personnel who try to get too chummy or treat you like a friend rather than an employer. This can be extremely dangerous. One late Latin American politician used to insist that his bodyguards not be excluded when he was drinking or carousing with women. Their job, however, was to protect the politician rather than join in the fun. Similarly, a widely known Hollywood star has permitted his bodyguards to become involved in his business affairs and even had one of them named associate producer of one of his movies. An individual who is thinking about business matters is unlikely to have the time or inclination to look after his employer's security properly.

Common sense. Bodyguards do not make you invincible. Your security still depends to a large extent on the common sense you exhibit with respect to living your life. Don't take unnecessary risks simply because you have bodyguards. Many people have been killed or taken hostage after their bodyguards were disposed of by terrorists. The fact that Aldo Moro, the late leader of Italy's Christian Democrats, had bodyguards didn't save him when he was grabbed by members of the Red Brigades.

Continuous training. Three words are associated with preparing your security detail: training, training, and more training.

Your bodyguards should constantly attempt to upgrade their skills. Time should be set aside each month for them to maintain their skills with firearms, to be briefed on new terrorist and other threats, to receive language training, and to keep up with developments regarding security technology. They should practice their skills in simulated incidents.

Periodically you should devote an afternoon to running through a number of ambush and kidnapping scenarios with your security detail. By working closely together, you and your security detail will learn to anticipate each other's reactions so that when a real problem occurs, you will not be at cross-purposes.

Choosing the Proper Equipment

Body armor. Your bodyguards should wear bulletproof vests (or other garments), as should you. You should insist that they wear such apparel at all times, since a member of your security detail is of no value to you with a bullet in his chest.

First aid kit. Your security detail should always have a first aid kit handy. The kit should contain, among other things, compress dressings and splints, charcoal in case you are poisoned, sutures and needles, antiseptic, possibly an oxygen mask and oxygen, and any medications that you or any member of your family requires.

Beepers. Members of your security detail should carry beepers so that you can summon them in an emergency.

Portable alarms. Although smoke detectors are generally required in U.S. hotels, when traveling abroad your security detail should carry portable fire alarms for your hotel rooms. In addition, portable door alarms are a good idea, as are intrusion devices such as contact and pressure alarms for windows and room access points. All these can be connected to an alarm in the room of a security staff member.

Scramblers. Portable scrambler systems are now available at very reasonable prices and generally ensure that no one can eavesdrop on your telephone conversations as long as a compatible scrambler is being used by the person on the other end of the line.

Walkie-talkies. Your bodyguards should be able to communicate with each other, and with you, via walkie-talkies.

Traveling with Your Bodyguards

Planning. Well before departure time, your protective detail should have mapped out your trip. They should have assembled street maps covering your proposed routes to and from airports, hotels, and appointments. They should have a list of emergency numbers in every city you plan to visit, including numbers of the fire and police departments and the hospitals. If you are a threatened person, a representative of your protective detail should consult in advance with local law enforcement agencies to determine local terrorist and criminal activity and to inform them that you will be visiting their city.

Traveling abroad. A member of your security detail should check with the U.S. Department of State regarding the latest travel advisories pertaining to your route. Once you are abroad, a member of your protective detail should call on the regional security officer (RSO) at the U.S. embassy to learn as much as possible about local threats to Americans. The RSO normally maintains good contact with local law enforcement authorities as well as the general population. If any trouble is brewing, he may know about it in advance.

Advancing a trip. If you have a large enough security staff, a member of your protective detail should travel ahead to scout out trouble. He should drive over any routes you anticipate taking at the hours you expect to be traveling them. There is nothing like a traffic jam or construction delay to disrupt your itinerary and your security arrangements.

Your security detail is not in any position to compel local authorities to look out for your safety. Whoever is advancing the trip should attempt to develop a cordial relationship with local law enforcement officials. If they offer assistance, he should coordinate your security arrangements with them but not rely exclusively on them for your safety.

Your security arrangements also should be coordinated with the security officer at the hotel where you are staying, but only after your advance man meets with the hotel manager. Be forewarned that many hotel security officers are tired old men, either ill-equipped for the job or eager to prove how much authority they carry in the hotel. Your security person should complain directly to the manager in the event that the hotel's security staff does not cooperate effectively or efficiently. The hotel should respond readily to requests regarding the identities of maids and other service personnel with whom you will come into contact, the location and layout of the room in which you will stay, and the identities, or at least nationalities, of nearby guests.

Note: To the extent possible, the member of your protective detail preceding you should be given the task of making preparations for your security, not performing routine duties best left to travel agents and secretaries.

Getting equipment through customs. Your security detail should make advance arrangements to get any equipment they need through customs. Even relatively mundane equipment such as walkie-talkies sometimes can cause problems. If there is any doubt about whether a particular piece of equipment will be a problem, leave it at home and lease it from a local security firm.

In this connection, contracting with a local security firm for some services may have many advantages. Personnel from such firms often are former law enforcement or military officers and thus not only are part of the old boy network but also generally maintain extensive local contacts that might come in handy. They usually know whom to contact to obtain various permits and the right names to drop to get the cooperation of local security forces.

In addition, remember that in most Western countries, your security personnel probably will be prohibited from carrying guns. If firepower is a must, a local security firm may be able to provide you with a contract bodyguard licensed to carry a weapon. In countries such as the United Kingdom, however, local security firms can rarely obtain firearms licenses. If the threat to you is serious enough, the government will assist in your arrangements.

Staying at a Hotel

Room location. In general, when you are staying in a hotel, the rooms on either side of yours are of concern. Your security detail should occupy both, or if you are traveling with only one guard, he should occupy one room and the other should be left vacant. If these options are not available, your security detail should make an effort to find out who occupies these rooms. If you are a threatened person, the rooms above and below yours should be checked for explosives.

Your room should be high enough to prevent ready access from the street but not so high as to be at risk in the event of a fire. Consider something between the third and seventh floors (remember, in many countries the first floor is called the ground floor and the first floor is really the second floor).

Exits. Locate the emergency exits at once. Also locate alternative elevators and staircases that could be used to facilitate your escape in an emergency.

Room service. If possible, have room service deliver food and drink to your bodyguard's room rather than to your own.

At the very least, have a bodyguard answer the door and remain in your room until the waiter has departed. If you are a threatened person, a member of your security detail might want to pat down the waiter outside the room. You also might consider asking the person with whom you place the room service order for the name and a brief description of the individual who will be delivering the order (to ensure that no one takes his or her place on the way to your room).

Telephone calls. Incoming telephone calls should be directed to your bodyguard's room to be screened. Callers should not be given any information about you or your room number by the hotel switchboard. Switchboard personnel should be instructed to contact the manager or hotel security chief if a caller inquires too persistently about you.

Maid service. After your room has been made up, a member of your security detail should check it over to make sure no bombs or other hazards have been introduced. He should make certain that window and door latches are tight and that no one is hiding in the closet or under the bed. In Latin America, maids sometimes leave the balcony door unlatched so that accomplices can sneak into the room and wait for the unsuspecting hotel guest to return, whereupon he is mugged.

Your valuables. Just because you have bodyguards is no reason to treat your valuables casually. Virtually all fine hotels offer safe deposit boxes to their guests for the storage of valuables. Use them. Your security detail has better things to do than guard your valuables and personal items. Moreover, you may simply invite trouble by leaving your valuables around.

Attending Social and Other Public Functions

Make your bodyguard's job as easy as possible. While it is your bodyguard's responsibility to anticipate the future, he is not clairvoyant. You can make his task easier by furnishing him with a list of your social functions and the appropriate apparel for each.

Check out all social functions. If you are a threatened person, your security detail will probably want to know the names of other guests at the parties to which you are invited. This is not only to ensure that Abu Nidal is not on the guest list, but also to identify other high-profile guests who might be targets of a terrorist or assassination attempt. For example, the U.S. or Israeli ambassador may be an obvious target. Your security detail also should investigate the amount of publicity the function has received, whether the guest list has been leaked to the media, and what security precautions the organizers of the event have taken.

Survey the premises. Your security detail should survey the premises in advance to discover any obvious security deficiencies. In addition, they should note the various entrances and exits and examine the parking area. They should identify a safe area to which you can be taken in case of trouble.

Take special precautions when making speeches. For small gatherings, take the same precautions you would for any social event. Should you be addressing a convention or large audience in an auditorium, however, more extensive security precautions are required. You should never rely completely on the security provided by the convention center management.

If you are a threatened person, the convention center should be swept in advance for explosives. Once it is declared clean, it should be secured until the event.

Most auditoriums and convention centers have a series of catwalks from which spotlights are directed at the stage. A sniper can conceal himself anywhere along them. Virtually all auditoriums also have platforms above the stage to service the myriad pulleys raising and lowering curtains and scenery, each providing a firing platform for a sniper. A sniper in either of these potential threat areas will probably be masked by the glare of the lights until the moment he fires. Thus, your security detail should make sure that someone patrols the catwalks and platforms and that the access points to them are guarded.

Some of your security people should be positioned directly in front of the stage or your podium. Others should stand in the wings, where they can watch the catwalks without being blinded by the lights and prevent anyone unauthorized from coming onstage. Note that many hotels and convention centers provide a bulletproof lectern or podium so that you can duck behind it if someone starts firing at you.

Dining with Your Bodyguards

Members of your security detail should feel comfortable in fine restaurants and be knowledgeable of everything from table manners to tipping.

Your safety comes before your bodyguard's stomach. Ideally, members of your security detail should take their meals when they are off duty. If that is not possible, they may dine at your table or an adjoining table. They should eat quickly and with a minimum of fuss so that they can devote full attention to your protection. If there is enough time, members of your security detail should stagger their meal schedules so that there will always be one or two individuals concentrating fully on your security.

Your protective detail is still on duty. Bodyguards should avoid distractions and temptations during their meals. They should not become engaged in conversation with others at the table, nor should they accept any wine or drinks offered them. They should be polite to everyone at the table but alert to everything going on around you.

Your car should always be ready. Your security detail should always have a car ready outside to evacuate you or rush you to the hospital. Try not to leave your car in the custody of parking attendants, who could tamper with it or park it where it is not readily accessible. Your driver should be prepared to spirit you away at a moment's notice. It is preferable that he wait with the car, and to this end, it is better if he brings a sandwich along with him.

Following Up a Visit

Insist that members of your security detail write letters of thanks to all who have aided in your protection. Not only will you leave a good impression, but you may need their assistance again at some time in the future.

8

Bombs and Explosives

Bombs are today the terrorist's weapon of choice. Not only are modern explosives more powerful than ever before, but the terrorist generally can be far from the scene when the bomb goes off, thus reducing his own risk of either injury or capture.

Bomb security is more than just the physical act of removing a package containing explosives found in your mail room. It is a sensible, two-pronged program of precautions and emergency procedures. Your precautions can limit the areas of vulnerability and the damage a bomb could inflict and may even cause the bomber to look elsewhere for an easier target. Advance precautions also will assist you in identifying a surreptitious bomb before it is detonated. Good emergency procedures will assist you in responding to an actual bomb emergency, either by evacuating the premises and disposing of the threat or by effectively dealing with the aftermath of a bomb attack.

External Security

Securing the perimeter. The first rule of preventing bomb attacks is to reduce the bomber's opportunity to get close to his target. The farther he is from your office or home, the less damage the explosive is likely to do. Consider the installation of fences, lighting, and sensors, as well as the use of guard patrols, to thwart infiltrators. High fences also may catch rocket-propelled grenades fired from outside and force them to detonate before they hit a building.

Preventing vehicle bombers. If you are living in a dangerous country, all vehicles approaching your factory or corporate headquarters should be inspected for explosives and weapons at a perimeter checkpoint. You might require all vehicles to park some distance away and shuttle occupants to their destinations in a minibus. If your firm has an underground garage, you might want to close it. It is not enough to restrict use of the garage to employees. In Beirut a bomb was planted in a secretary's car without her knowledge and radio-detonated when she entered her embassy's compound.

In the event that a vehicle runs or breaks through the checkpoint, you can take other steps to stop it before it reaches its target. Low bridges, which can be constructed simply by putting a steel I beam across the road, will block larger vehicles and permit only cars to pass underneath, thus reducing the amount of explosives that can be transported to the target. Speed bumps will slow down a hostile vehicle, as will a winding road designed like a slalom course or a road with sharp right and left angle turns. Chicanes and slalomlike roads may have the added advantage of breaking the hostile driver's concentration. Studies have shown that this, in turn, is likely to undermine the driver's resolution to carry out an attack.

In addition, pop-up barriers, tire-puncturing devices, rising bollards, nets, crash beams, tank traps, and pits that open up in the road can be used to stop hostile vehicles. To reduce the damage if the hostile vehicle reaches the target building, you may want to block the front entrance with a heavy truck or armored vehicle. This was routinely done in Vietnam, and had the U.S. Marines in Beirut taken this precaution in 1983, the explosives-laden truck would not have been able to detonate in the lobby of the headquarters/barracks building, perhaps reducing the number of casualties.

Protecting windows. Windows overlooking the street—particularly large picture windows—could admit a gasoline bomb, grenade, or rocket. Vulnerable windows should be fitted with bullet-resistant glass or receive some kind of window treatment and be covered with grenade screens.

Removing rubbish. Rubbish lying about is not only untidy and unsightly, but it can easily conceal an explosive device. A bomb search is a time-consuming and dangerous task if all garbage cans must be examined, paper cartons opened up, and half-filled paint cans checked. Instruct your maintenance staff to keep the property clean of rubbish and debris. This will make the bomber's job much more difficult.

Removing decorative shrubs and ornaments. Remove decorative shrubs and ornaments that could hide a bomb. Examine all ventilation ducts, drainpipes and rain gutters, and other places where a bomb could be hidden.

Access Control

Detection devices. A variety of detection devices are available to identify the presence of explosives. Bomb sniffers that detect traces of nitrogen oxide are the most sophisticated. Metal detectors also are useful because bombs are almost impossible to construct without some metal components. Detonators generally have metal cases, and percussion and electrical fuses are made of metal. Metal detectors will, however, give off many false alarms. Packages containing stapled material or those bound with metal fasteners will regularly trip detectors and have to be inspected. Note that a number of companies manufacture relatively reliable desktop bomb detectors that can be used to screen incoming mail.

Physical searches. In areas of high threat, you might consider pat down or physical search of employees and guests entering the premises. Such searches often cause resentment and are generally very time-consuming.

Hand luggage and purses. Hand luggage and purses should be x-rayed or physically searched for weapons and explosives. Be aware that such searches are not foolproof. A bomb may be disassembled into unrecognizable parts and concealed inside a camera or tape recorder. You may want to instruct your security personnel to switch on tape recorders and peer through camera eyepieces to make sure they are the genuine article.

X-ray operators should pay particular attention to the outline of clocks, wires, watches, batteries, switches, springs, and any item that shows up as dense material. Bottles and cans could be part of an incendiary device, and these should not be allowed in the building without first being checked by hand.

X-ray operators tend to get bored quickly. Impress upon them the importance of their job and see to it that they are well supervised. A recent study found that security personnel manning x-ray machines at U.S. airports missed 20 percent of all weapons being smuggled through.

Loading dock. Be sure to establish good security procedures at your loading dock. In dangerous regions of the world, everything from cafeteria supplies to bulk paper should be checked. Your guards should scrutinize all vehicles, drivers, and loads that arrive at the loading dock. Use a mirror on a long pole to look underneath delivery vehicles. Delivery vehicles also should be kept under surveillance to make sure the driver doesn't attempt to plant a bomb somewhere on his way in or out.

Letter Bombs

Screen all mail to detect either metal or explosives. If screening devices are impractical or too expensive, note the following danger signs:

- There is no return address.
- The person or firm indicated on the return address is not recognizable.
- The name and address are composed of letters clipped from newspapers or magazines.
- The postmark is from a known trouble spot (most often the Middle East).
- The letter or parcel has a dead feeling, such as putty or clay would give it, rather than the spring and flexibility of a sheaf of papers.
- The letter or parcel feels lopsided or heavy for its size.
- The letter or parcel has greasy patches or looks as though something is soaking it from the inside. (Explosives have a tendency to sweat.)
- The letter or parcel has a smell similar to marzipan or almonds (indicative of some explosives).
- The parcel has some unusual feature, such as the contents appear to have been inserted from the side so that the recipient will detonate the package when he opens it from the top.
- The outline of a hairspring trip mechanism resembling a small coin can be seen on the envelope or parcel.

Note that the most sophisticated letter bombs are thinner and more compact than ever before and therefore may demonstrate none of the outward manifestations noted above. The only way to discover the real nature of such letters and parcels is to screen them through an x-ray or explosives detector.

What to do if you discover a bomb in the mail. Call the police or your security office at once. Do not handle the suspicious parcel or envelope. If you are already holding it, carry it gently to a corner, place it on the floor, and evacuate the area in an orderly fashion. If you are at risk or have been threatened, you might consider buying a professional bomb blanket, such as those used by explosives ordnance demolition (EOD) specialists. A bomb blanket is a heavy blanket made of bomb-resistant material designed to absorb much of the blast and to cut down on shrapnel.

How to handle bomb threats received by mail. If you receive a bomb threat by mail, place the letter in a plastic bag, taking care to handle it as little as possible. Then call the police. Police forensics specialists can then go over the letter for clues.

Building Security

Ducts. All air-conditioning and ventilation ducts should be covered with grilles to make it more difficult for bombs to be placed inside. Grilles also will allow for visual inspections. Be cautious of installing suspended ceilings where explosive devices could be hidden.

Rest rooms. Be careful about giving visitors access to rest rooms and other areas where they are free of supervision. A bomb can be assembled in a toilet stall and then planted in the trash can by the sink.

Stairwells. Stairwells with exterior exits are always dangerous. If the building has elevators, the stairwells tend not to be used much. Stairwells should not be accessible from the outside and should be inspected on a regular basis by security personnel.

Sprinklers and alarms. Remember to install systems not just to deter a bomber, but also to minimize the damage he can do. Fire-suppressant systems and alarms should be installed, especially in rooms housing vital records or machinery.

Closed-circuit television (CCTV). You may want to install closed-circuit television cameras to monitor out-of-the-way areas. These cameras also are useful for keeping track of a large number of people. It is important to remember, however, that closed-circuit cameras are only as good as the people watching the monitors.

Critical Zones. While routine bomb precautions should be mandatory for your entire plant or office complex, you might consider designating certain areas (such as those containing vital machinery or fuel) as critical zones. Such areas would be made off-limits to all employees except those with special clearance.

Briefings. If you live in a dangerous country, your security chief should conduct periodic briefings for company employees regarding bomb threats and attacks. He should establish procedures for evacuating the plant or building in the event of a serious bomb threat and make certain that everyone knows where they are supposed to go. He also should review building exits and designate certain people to act as evacuation marshals. All new employees should be required to attend such a briefing as part of their orientation.

Bombs and Bomb Threats

Strange objects. The easiest bomb to plant is one concealed in a lunch pail, briefcase, or shopping bag left in your waiting room or some other obvious area. Generally, someone will notice a strange object sitting on the floor with no apparent owner and alert a member of your staff. Before sounding the alarm, make certain that the parcel is actually unattended. Whatever you do, don't touch a suspected bomb.

False alarms. If your staff is characterized by a high level of security awareness, be prepared for all sorts of false alarms. People will have a tendency to see bombs everywhere. Nevertheless, don't punish them or discourage them from questioning suspicious items. If you do, they are likely to give every suspicious item the benefit of the doubt, and when a real bomb appears, they will ignore it.

Bomb threats. A bombing may be preceded by a telephone call or other warning. Your receptionists and telephone operators should be briefed on how to handle bomb threats. Although most bomb threats are hoaxes, given the possible results of a real bomb attack, every threat should be treated as though it were genuine.

Whoever takes the call should stay calm, a skill that can be taught by means of simulated bomb threats and training exercises. First and foremost, the operator must attempt to get the time and location of the threatened attack. Nothing else matters until these two questions are answered.

If the caller refuses to divulge this information, your operator might try a variety of techniques to get him or her to talk. The operator can pretend to have difficulty hearing the caller because of office noise or a bad connection. Encouraging the caller to talk may loosen his or her lips, and he or she may reveal more than intended. If all else fails, the operator can refuse to believe the caller or take the threat seriously until more information is forthcoming. This is a dangerous technique and should be used only as a last resort.

Once the necessary information is acquired, the operator should try to keep the caller on the line. The operator should listen for any background noises, speech characteristics, or other things that could be used later to identify the caller.

If bomb threats are frequent, you should consider hooking a tape recorder to your telephone system. The recorder could then be activated in the event of a bomb threat.

Evacuation Procedures

Plan and rehearse evacuating your building or facility. Designate someone who has the authority to order an evacuation in your absence as well as a backup for that person. During a bomb scare is no time to improvise.

Don't take bomb threats lightly. If you get a bomb threat, ignore grousing from employees and others who might be inconvenienced. It is better to be safe than sorry. Remember, the failure to evacuate a structure could lead to serious liability problems if there actually is a bomb.

Avoid panic. The order to evacuate ideally should be given by office supervisors. A general warning issued over the public address system could easily start a panic. Asking people to leave because of a gas or water leak is one way to clear a building without starting a stampede.

Open doors and windows. If you use a fire alarm to evacuate the building, people may shut all the doors and windows in an effort to reduce the oxygen supply to the fire. This is good practice in the event of a fire but not if you are dealing with a bomb. Instruct employees to open all doors and windows to dissipate the blast. Also tell them to shut down machinery or dangerous equipment that could add to your problems later.

Never trust a terrorist. Remember, the bomber may have second-guessed you by planting the bomb in the area to which people are evacuated. The IRA has done this on a number of occasions. If possible, your evacuation site should be in an open area, away from structures and objects where a bomb could be hidden. Your security staff should check the evacuation site as quickly as possible for bombs.

Keep rubberneckers away. Your employees may be curious and try to venture close to the building to watch the action. Don't let them. Maintain a strict cordon.

While your security staff should be attending to the bomb threat and the crowd, you may want to designate someone to take pictures of the crowd. Some bombers are fascinated by their own handiwork and like to look on from the crowd.

Check for terrorist infiltrators. Terrorists may attempt to mingle with your employees after the all clear has been sounded and people are permitted to return to work. This is often an easy way to get past security guards. To guard against this threat, have your security staff check the identification badges of all who reenter the building.

Take special care at hazardous product facilities. If your company is engaged in manufacturing chemicals or other potentially hazardous products, any bomb evacuation should be coordinated with local authorities, especially fire and police units. They may want to take the precaution of evacuating nearby businesses and residences.

Call the fire department first. If you are going to rely on the local authorities to conduct the bomb search, generally it is best to alert the fire department first. They are more likely to respond quickly.

Participate in the bomb search. Have someone familiar with the layout of the building or facility accompany each bomb search team. Keys to all doors and lockers, as well as floor plans and architectural drawings, should be readily available.

Beware of bomb hoaxes. Terrorists or political agitators may use bomb hoaxes for a variety of reasons, such as diverting attention from a robbery or break-in, conducting industrial espionage, instilling panic, lowering productivity, causing employee injuries during the evacuation, demoralizing employees, or simply attempting to make you and your company look foolish or inept. An effective evacuation plan will help minimize such consequences.

Consider different approaches to persistent bomb threats. To prevent your employees from going around the bend with aggravation, you might consider some alternatives to a full evacuation of your business or facility. A localized evacuation may be warranted in some cases. Alternatively, you may want to ask your employees to search their work areas for suspected bombs. As each should be familiar with the floor space and objects in his or her area, he or she should be able to notice anything that is out of place.

Employee searches will reduce the sense that employees are having their turf violated. No one likes being pushed out of his or her office by a uniformed guard who proceeds to root through his or her desk and files.

Bomb Searches

Have a plan. Before sending people out willy-nilly in the hope that one of them will stumble over the bomb, plan a careful search pattern. Check to see if a bomb could have been planted by a visitor or could have arrived in a recent shipment. Any area where visitors congregate, such as waiting rooms or rest rooms, is a likely place for a bomb.

Turn off all alarms. Most internal alarms should be turned off prior to the search. The search teams will already be on edge without being further aggravated by someone tripping an alarm.

Move through the facility slowly. Beware of booby traps. They may be triggered by trip wires or vibration switches or attached to doors or pressure-sensitive plates. No one should touch anything that looks out of place, but instead should mark it for the bomb squad.

The search teams should be alert for anything that looks recently disturbed: loose floorboards and carpeting; freshly plastered walls; recently disturbed ground; sawdust, brick dust, or wood chips. Such areas should be marked for the bomb squad but never disturbed.

Don't bunch up. Members of the search team should spread out in order to minimize the chance that a bomb detonated by one member will inflict casualties on others. They should be deployed in alternate rooms, with no more than two people to a room.

Listen. Many bombs use an alarm clock mechanism. The first order of business is for the search teams to rely on their sense of hearing. They must attempt to screen out background noises and detect the telltale ticking of an alarm clock.

Start at the perimeter. The search teams should go around the walls first, working their way to the center of the room. They should start at opposite ends of the room and work back toward each other.

Check under tables. Look for bombs taped underneath tables and chairs. Check all chairs for signs of tears and lumps within the cushions.

Check desk drawers and closets. Keys should be available for all locked drawers and cabinets.

Check suspended ceilings. If the room has a suspended ceiling, you may have to investigate the space above it. Pay sharp attention to signs of tampering or acoustic tiles that don't fit right. Examine ducts and wiring. Look for tool marks on air ducts, electrical trunks, and control boxes; these could be indicative of forced entry.

Check elevator shafts. Elevator shafts end in a pit beneath the lowest floor; this will have to be checked. A security officer should sit atop the car, riding up one floor at a time to look for explosives with a flashlight. He should check the counterweights as they come down, as well as the winding machinery at the top.

Assume the worst. You should never assume that only one device has been planted. Should you find one device, don't abandon the search until the entire building or facility has been inspected.

Mark areas that have been inspected. This will prevent inadvertent duplication of effort.

Take frequent breaks. Search teams should take periodic breaks. Searching for a bomb is a tense and tiring job that demands total concentration. If searchers get too weary, they may overlook the obvious or not recognize a bomb when they see it.

Turn off walkie-talkies. This will help prevent a bomb from being detonated by radio signals.

Bomb (suppression) blanket. Should you find a bomb or suspicious object, carefully drape a bomb blanket, made of blast-resistant material, over the object until the bomb squad arrives. If the bomb goes off, the bomb blanket will reduce shrapnel and lessen the blast effects unless it is a very powerful device. You can protect valuable equipment nearby with sandbags and fire-suppressant foam. Never forget, however, that any solid object placed near a bomb will become a projectile or, worse, shrapnel in the event of an explosion.

Move a bomb only if absolutely necessary. If, for some extraordinary reason, you judge it necessary to move the bomb away from a door it is blocking or from proximity to irreplaceable equipment, do it the right way. Don't pick it up. Instead, attach a rope or heavy nylon cord to the object with adhesive tape. Then get as far away from the bomb as possible and pull it away from the critical area, always maintaining a safe distance between yourself and the bomb.

Bomb Checks before Public Events

Bomb-sniffing dogs. Highly trained bomb-sniffing dogs are generally the best way to ferret out explosives in a large auditorium or convention hall. Dogs, however, are not infallible. A visual search also should be made of the premises.

Stage. The area beneath the stage is often used for storage and props or is interspersed with crawl spaces to service electrical cables. It should be checked thoroughly.

Orchestra pit. The orchestra pit may be on a hydraulic lift or have its own storage area. Both will have to be checked.

Ventilation system. All theaters are fitted with extensive air-circulation systems. In many cases, these are readily accessible to unauthorized people. The ventilation system should be thoroughly inspected. It may even be necessary to have someone crawl through the ducts to make sure they are safe.

Area above the stage. The area above the stage is a jungle of fixtures used to raise and lower scenery. There are many places to hide a bomb, although it is probably not the most effective place to put a device. Similarly, the catwalks above and flanking the auditorium are not particularly effective places to hide a bomb and can be given only a cursory examination.

Dressing room. Always search the dressing room before a potential target uses it.

Seats. Check beneath the seats. In addition, examine seat cushions for cuts or bulges indicating that something has been inserted inside.

Bombs aboard Corporate Aircraft

Take precautions. A number of corporate aircraft have been blown out of the sky by bombs, so you should take certain precautions. Corporate aircraft should be stored in secure areas and fitted with alarms. If you are in the midst of labor strife or have other reasons to feel threatened, consider having around-the-clock guards to watch the aircraft.

Remove the plane from the hangar. If you have reason to suspect that a bomb may have been secreted aboard the plane, the threatened aircraft should be towed out of the hangar and the bomb search should be conducted in a relatively deserted area. A hangar full of other aircraft, fuel, and lubricants is no place to conduct a bomb search unless you have no other choice.

Remove and check all baggage. If there is baggage aboard, it should be checked first. Once the baggage has been removed, the passengers, if they are available, should point out their bags. A leftover bag may indicate that the would-be bomber mixed his bag with the rest of the luggage. If there is no left-over bag, all luggage should be opened and carefully inspected.

Check the aircraft's exterior, then move inside.

Check the most accessible areas first. Search the lavatory and cabinets, then the seat cushions and any other area where a bomb could have been hidden. Check for bombs in the shaft that runs the length of the plane, generally beneath the center aisle, where control cables are located. When inspecting machinery spaces, remember that a device need not be very large if it is designed simply to destroy vital cables, wiring, or instruments needed to control the aircraft.

Include both security and maintenance people on the inspection. A plane is a very complex piece of machinery, and only a trained aircraft mechanic or engineer may be able to distinguish a bomb from some vital piece of equipment. Remember that a clumsy bomb search may do more harm than the bomb itself by disrupting or impairing the aircraft.

Car Bombs

A car bomb can be rigged to anything that moves or through which an electrical current passes. For example, bombs can be wired to the ignition, headlights, or interior lights. They can be wired to the vehicle's seats and doors, set off by turning the steering wheel, or actuated by tilt switches that detonate when you go around a bend. Bombs also can be detonated by remote control, using a walkie-talkie, a toy airplane remote control unit, or a beeper system. Bombs can be set to explode by clockwork mechanisms or fuses. They can be placed in the gasoline tank, next to the fire wall, in the wheel wells, or inside the headrests. Besting a determined car bomber will take some effort on your part.

Don't make the bomber's job easy. Park your vehicle in a well-lighted, well-supervised area. Consider having it rigged with alarms. Admittedly, a soap dish bomb with a tilt switch can be attached beneath your car's gas tank in a matter of seconds. The bomber can pretend to tie his shoelace, pull the bomb from beneath his jacket, and stick the device underneath the car or in a wheel well. Explosives wired to the ignition will take more doing, however, and can be accomplished only when the vehicle is left unsecured for a long period of time.

Conduct an external bomb check. If your vehicle is well secured, the bomber must plant the device somewhere on the vehicle's exterior, where it will be relatively easy to locate. Walk around the vehicle. Check the wheel wells, tail pipes, and under the gas tank. Look for anything suspicious—any wires, electrical or duct tape, or other object stuck to the frame.

Do a more complete search if the vehicle has been left unattended. Check doors and trunk locks for signs of tampering. Any tool marks will indicate that someone has tried to force his way into your vehicle. Check the inside of the car through the window; look for strange packages or objects that may be protruding from under the seats or dashboard.

Consider buying a remote control starting device. A number of these devices are available to allow you to start your vehicle from a safe distance.

What Do Bombs Look Like?

Bombs come in all shapes and sizes. If you see anything that looks unusual or out of place, it is a good idea to bring it to the attention of the bomb squad.

Nitroglycerin. Nitroglycerin is an oily, colorless liquid. Do not expect to find it often because it is very unstable and can be detonated by shock. Not many terrorists want to carry it around.

Dynamite. Dynamite is an absorbent material soaked in nitroglycerin. It is then wrapped in waxed paper. As it ages, it begins to seep drops of liquid nitroglycerin and becomes far less stable. As the nitroglycerin starts seeping out of the sticks, it makes a greasy mess and is very dangerous to handle. Many other types of explosives also sweat, and wet stains on a package are a good clue that there might be explosives inside.

Phosphorus bombs. Phosphorus, which looks like yellowed wax, is used in many incendiary devices. It is an ideal arsonist's tool because it bursts into flames when exposed to air. It can be mixed with carbon disulfide to keep it inert, then splashed on some flammable material. When the carbon disulfide evaporates, the phosphorus ignites. Since no detonator or timing device is needed, phosphorus-based incendiaries will be difficult to spot.

Black powder. In commercially produced form, black powder appears as small, flat, shiny black or gray grains or flakes. In improvised form, it appears as black, yellow, or white powder or crystals. Black powder is often used in pipe bombs. Smokeless gunpowder is somewhat more powerful than black powder. Note: The flash from AG1-B flashbulbs will normally be enough of an initiator to detonate black powder.

TNT. TNT is usually found in creamy yellow blocks.

Plastic explosives. Plastic (or plastique) is the most common terrorist explosive, chiefly because of its stability, its power, and the fact that it can be shaped into practically any form. Semtex, manufactured by the Eastern Bohemian Chemical Works in Czechoslovakia, has been used in virtually every Arab letter bomb to date and is easily recognized by its bright orange color.

Very little plastic is required to produce a devastating explosion. In tests conducted at the FBI facility at Quantico, Virginia, half an ounce of C4, a U.S.-produced plastic explosive, was enough to make a huge upright freezer disintegrate. The same amount could easily be rolled out in a flat sheet and secreted in a mailing envelope.

Incendiaries. Any highly flammable material, including gasoline and brake fluid, can be used to make an incendiary device. Be careful how such materials are stored in your plant or workplace. If flammable materials are stockpiled in abundance, a small explosion may be enough to trigger a raging inferno.

Improvised explosives. As any bomb squad member will tell you, improvised explosives are the most dangerous of all because you never know what you are dealing with or the skill level of the bomb maker. A few grains of black powder left in the threads of the device may be enough to detonate it.

Detonators and blasting caps. In many cases, the presence of a detonator or blasting cap may be the only clue that an object is a bomb. Explosives are commonly detonated by a smaller blast from an initiator, such as a detonator or blasting cap. Blasting caps, which are generally made of several layers of different explosives, come in a variety of strengths, but even the weakest can be lethal to a human being.

Blasting caps may be either electrical or nonelectrical. Electrical caps are most often hooked to a power source, such as a standard D battery, by means of two solid copper wires. Electrical blasting caps are usually bright metallic cylinders of copper or aluminum, each about the diameter of a pencil and six inches long. Nonelectrical caps (fuse or pyrotechnic caps) have a time or safety fuse on one end. Once the fuse is lit, it will burn until it reaches the cap, detonating the most sensitive explosive, which in turn causes the cap to explode. Often the fuse is colored by the manufacturer to indicate the speed at which it burns.

Activators/power sources. Every bomb requires some kind of power source to activate the initiator. Electrical batteries are the most popular power source, but the new generation of very small, flat batteries makes it even easier for the bomb maker to disguise his handiwork.

Fuses. Fuses are simply switches required to activate an explosive device. The three main types are time delay, physical action, and environmental. Good examples of time delay fuses are chemical pencils, a few feet of a stringlike fuse that burns, or something as simple as an alarm clock with wires attached to each hand and leading to the explosive. When the two hands meet and the electrical contacts touch, the circuit is completed and the bomb explodes. Time delay fuses may take the form of two chemicals that ignite when they are mixed together or explode after a certain period of time. Another type of time delay fuse uses acid, which eats through wire or solder and causes the jaws of a clothespin to snap shut, completing a circuit.

Physical action fuses are things such as trip wires, pressure-sensitive devices, and commercially available intrusion detection sensors. In other words, the action of placing pressure on something or relieving pressure detonates the bomb.

Environmental fuses require some change in the environment—temperature, barometric pressure, altitude, light, atmospheric pressure—to set off the explosive device.

Final Caveat

Remember, untrained individuals should never try to deactivate a bomb, no matter what the type. The device may be rigged with a booby trap. Once you identify a bomb, clear the area and wait for the bomb disposal experts to arrive. If it is feasible, remove anything that could become an incendiary or missile if the device should explode.

9

Kidnapping

ONCE among the rarest of crimes, kidnapping for ransom or for political reasons has increased dramatically in recent years. Convictions for criminal kidnappings in the United States are up fivefold in the past quarter century. In many countries, especially in the Third World, the problem is even worse, as the number of political kidnappings has reached epidemic proportions.

Despite the fact that many companies and individuals have responded with beefed-up security precautions, kidnappers suffer from no shortage of soft targets who have little, if any, protection. The suggestions below are designed to help you survive a kidnapping ordeal in the unfortunate event that you should be a victim.

Choosing a Target

"It can never happen to me." Forget these words. Excise them from your vocabulary. The fact is, it *can* happen to you. Time after time, kidnap victims later explain that they didn't take security precautions because they rejected the idea that anyone would regard them as a potential target.

You don't have to be rich or powerful to be a target. A few years ago, authorities in a Third World country knocked over a terrorist safe house and found a list of potential kidnap victims. In every instance where the potential victim was observing at least some security precautions; the name had been stricken from the list. Since most top officials and corporate officers have some kind of security, kidnappers increasingly are snatching mid-level employees who are accessible and have not taken elaborate security precautions. U.S. general James Dozier, kidnapped in Italy and held by terrorists for six weeks, was not the top target of the Red Brigades; in fact, his name was near the bottom of the list. Looking back on his experience, Dozier admits that he was foolish not to perceive any threat to himself or his family.

The Abduction Phase

If you resist, you may be killed. The kidnappers want you alive, not dead, but if you resist forcefully, you increase the likelihood that you may be killed or injured. Eventually, nearly all kidnap victims are released in exchange for a ransom or other consideration. Remember, if they wanted you dead, they would have killed you outright, not kidnapped you. Thus, you should examine the possible consequences of resistance very carefully.

The experience will be unpleasant, at least initially. You will probably be treated very roughly until the abduction phase is over and the kidnappers begin to settle down. At the outset, they will want you to do exactly what they say, and the best way to ensure this is to fill you with fear.

The kidnappers will probably blindfold you or place a hood over your head to prevent you from summoning help or seeing where you are being taken. The blindfold also ensures that you cannot see their faces. Unless you plan on escaping (generally not a good idea), do not spend a lot of time trying to wriggle out of your blindfold. Should you be successful and see their faces, they may feel compelled to kill you rather than exchange you for a ransom.

Captives are sometimes drugged. Many kidnappers believe that their hostages are easier to manage if they have been drugged. Although it may be little comfort, remember that you are their bargaining chip and they don't want anything to happen to you. The injection or the pills being forced into your mouth will probably be a sedative.

You may be bound with tape. Kidnappers frequently bind their victims like mummies to move them from one location to the next without incident. A tape-bound victim can be stuffed in a car trunk or box without fear that he or she will thump on the container in an effort to alert the authorities.

Try to remember sounds, scents, and other things that might later help the authorities discover the kidnappers' hideout. You also might want to try and record the passage of time. This will help give police some idea of the distance you were taken, although some kidnappers counter this by driving around in circles for a while to throw off your sense of time and distance.

When the sister of a prominent Central American businessman was kidnapped, although bound and blindfolded, during her captivity, she remembered a number of things that later made it possible to find the house where she had been held. Among these were the flight path of aircraft overhead, a passing religious procession, and the scent of a bakery.

Consider some prearranged signals that might provide information to the authorities. You may have the opportunity to speak with a member of your family on the telephone or by letter. A good hostage negotiator will always ask to speak to the hostage to make sure he or she is alive before paying a ransom. An innocuous-sounding phrase inserted into your conversation may give authorities a vital clue that will help them locate you.

A prominent landowner kidnapped in Central America also was one of the finest chess players in the country. He was able to provide a clue to the identity of his abductors when he wrote a letter, at the direction of his kidnappers, to his family attesting to his health and well-being. In the letter he noted that he had "played three games of chess and won one." One of the few people capable of beating him in the entire country was a leftist university professor, and it was later learned that he was involved in the abduction. The authorities did not react quickly enough to save the man's life, however.

Generally, the attempt to send a carefully veiled signal or clue to authorities is extremely dangerous. If the attempt is discovered, the kidnappers are likely to deal severely with you. Moreover, unless the signal is prearranged, there is no assurance that your family or the authorities will understand your message.

Don't shoot off your mouth. It may well be that your company or family has effective plans for securing your release in the event that you are kidnapped. If this is so, do not brag about it to your captors. Even a general smugness on your part may alert them that something is in the works. If your rescuers drop in, make certain that they arrive unannounced.

Interrogation

The "good guy, bad guy" routine. This is a standard interrogation technique. One interrogator will badger and harass you, doing his best to frighten and intimidate you. After he has gone, another interrogator will take his place. The second interrogator will be pleasant and sympathetic. He may offer you a cigarette and inquire how you are being treated. He may even apologize for the first man's behavior. Soon he will offer to be your protector. "Don't worry," he will assure you. "I will keep him from hurting you." Then the other shoe will drop. "Just give me a little information that I can use to show him that you are cooperating. You have to trust me."

Interrogation tricks. A common interrogation ruse is for the captors to show the victim a stack of files and tell him they already know all about him. Just confirm a few details, they urge, to show us you are willing to cooperate.

When there is more than one victim, a variation of this trick is to separate the prisoners. Later, you will be told that one of the other prisoners has already told them all about you and that resistance on your part is futile.

Your captors also might try to play on your emotions, taunting you or speaking of your family in an effort to provoke an outburst during which you will give something away.

The "prove that you are not" scenario. The interrogator walks into the room, flips through a dossier, and says matter-of-factly, "So, Mr. Smith, how long have you worked for the CIA?" You frantically protest that you are an engineer with Company X and have never worked for the CIA. "If that is the case," the interrogator responds, "then tell us about the work you are doing." In a desperate attempt to prove your innocence, you describe your company's business activities and thereby hand the terrorists everything they want to know. Be wary of such ploys.

Outsmarting the interrogator. Although you can rarely outsmart the interrogator, if you must try, evaluate your past performance in high-stress environments. How did you do in exams, during jobs interviews, and in crisis situations? Whether or not you can put up a good front is something you will have to decide for youself, but the best advice generally is to be truthful. A skilled interrogator usually will trip up someone who is lying. Without a well-planned and well-rehearsed story, the interrogator probably will see through you in a very short time. If you appear to be truthful and your story stands up under cross-examination, you may be able to withhold certain critical pieces of information, the disclosure of which could potentially harm others, without anyone being the wiser.

Remember that once you begin talking, it will be difficult for you to stop. Skilled interrogators will trap you with your own statements. They will ask you to repeat your story over and over, calling attention to any inconsistency, no matter how minor, from one version to the next. They will attempt to wear you down.

Whatever you do, pace yourself. Think before you speak. Do not rush your response. Neither you nor your interrogator has any other appointments.

Small minds. Size up your interrogators. How sophisticated are they? Do they appreciate subtleties? Are they simply thugs? The best advice this author ever got, before he was detained in a Third World dictatorship, was "If you get into trouble, remember that they have small minds." In other words, you may benefit from telling them what they want to hear. Agree with them without fawning over them. Maintain your dignity, but show flexibility and understanding of their point of view. Hostility on your part will most assuredly produce hostility in return.

Retaliation. Avoid the urge to make your interrogator several inches shorter and a whole lot uglier. Any effort to resist violently will rebound to your detriment. While you may get a moment's gratification, the kidnappers will make you pay. You are better off enduring the interrogator's taunts and slanders without trying to retaliate.

Physical torture. It is unlikely that you will be tortured, but if you are, some experts suggest that you can hold up under torture if you think constantly of those who will be put in peril by your statements. It may give you some comfort to know that you are likely to survive and ultimately will be released. When you are undergoing torture, it is wise to focus all of your thoughts and concentration on something other than the pain.

Few people can withstand prolonged torture without breaking. Thus, there is no shame in giving in to modern forms of physical duress. It is recommended that you not cave in immediately, for your interrogators will probably lose all respect for someone who tells everything even before he or she is subjected to abuse. Should your interrogators lose respect for you as a person, they may make your captivity even worse.

Captivity

Try to understand your role as a hostage. You have probably heard of the Stockholm syndrome, also known as traumatic bonding. This is the process whereby hostages begin to identify with their captors. The term *Stockholm syndrome* was coined after bank robbers in Sweden barricaded themselves in a vault with a number of hostages. The four hostages ultimately developed a peculiar affinity for their captors, later standing up for them after they surrendered to the police. One woman even divorced her husband and married one of the bank robbers.

Psychiatrists explain that during a hostage ordeal, it is common for terrorists and hostages to begin commiserating with each other. Just as submissive figures often become dependent on more dominant personalities, the powerless hostage grows dependent on his or her captors and may come to share their point of view or to regard the authorities as somehow antagonistic to both the terrorists and himself or herself.

Be cognizant of the fact that abduction casts you in a very dependent role. Your survival hangs on the whim of the terrorists. Understand these feelings of dependency and empathy toward your abductors and resist them. Talk to your fellow captives, if there are any, and develop bonds with them. *They* are your comrades, not the terrorists. Be on the lookout for signs of the Stockholm syndrome in others and help them to deal with such feelings. Keep their spirits up. Remind them that your chances of survival are great. Insist that they keep their composure and their dignity.

Try to develop a rapport with your captors. During the siege of a Dutch train, one of the captives was told by the terrorists that he was to be executed. He asked for a few moments to leave a message for his family. By the time the terrorists had listened to the story of his troubled family life, they were so emotionally involved that they found it impossible to kill him. He had transcended the role of hostage and became, in their eyes, another human being.

By showing the terrorists your human side, perhaps with pictures of your wife and family, you may make it more difficult for them to abuse you. Some terrorist groups have recognized this problem and provide courses on how to prevent becoming involved with captives. Guards are not allowed to talk to their captives except when necessary. They are rotated on a regular basis to make it more difficult for them to form attachments to their captives. Guards also work in pairs so that they can keep an eye on each other.

Don't assume that you can reason with terrorists and win them over. Avoid political discussions; you may only antagonize your captors. Nevertheless, try to be a good listener. A hostage in Latin America won over the most vicious of his captors by listening for hours to his mediocre poetry.

Don't offer advice. Should your captors accept your suggestion and it fails, you are likely to be blamed. One of the few exceptions to the rule occurred in 1980 when U.S. ambassador Diego Asencio and a number of other diplomats were taken hostage at the Dominican Republic's embassy in Bogota, Colombia, by M-19 terrorists. When it became apparent to Asencio that the terrorists weren't making any progress in their negotiations, he attributed it to their stridency and negotiating style and offered to help. "After all," he later recalled, "as a diplomat I was a professional negotiator." With Asencio's help, a solution to the standoff was ultimately crafted, which resulted in freedom for Asencio and the others.

Behave as though you are always under observation. After all, you probably will be. Accept the loss of privacy and learn to live with it. Also remember that your kidnappers may secretly tape all your conversations and interrogation sessions so that they can later use your comments against you.

Maintain your dignity. Next to your freedom, this is the most important thing your captors will try to take from you. You probably will be kept in squalid conditions. Your clothes may be confiscated, and it is not unusual for kidnappers to force you to live in your underwear. The food may be almost inedible, and you might be required to eat it with your fingers. There is every reason to believe that you will be humiliated and bullied. Don't grovel, beg, or give in. Go about your daily activities with cooperative resignation without being either too eager or too reluctant.

Eat everything you are given, even if it is rancid and unpalatable. It is vital that you keep up your strength, and to do so you will have to eat. If you develop intestinal trouble, drink as many liquids as possible to avoid dehydration.

Locate a safe haven in your prison. If security forces come in shooting, you will want to find cover as quickly as possible. Think in advance about where you will take shelter in the event of a rescue effort. If there is no cover, hit the floor when you hear the sound of shooting or any other disturbance.

Exercise regularly. Just as you would in everyday life, try to keep in shape. Do your best to improvise a workout. Isometric exercises and jogging in place are a good bet. If your captors will provide you with a length of rope, consider jumping rope. Push-ups, squat thrusts, toe touches, and knee bends require little space.

Combat loneliness. Ask your captors for reading material. Read as much as you can to ward off the isolation blues. If you run out of new reading material, try memorizing sections of books or magazines that you have. Devise mental games. Whatever you do, don't let your mind be idle because that's when depression sets in.

Adapt to your environment. As bad as it may be, be thankful that you are still alive and will probably one day be free again. Never lose sight of this fact. When the British ambassador to Brazil was abducted some years ago, he always maintained that he was still ambassador and that his cell was his embassy. As such, he demanded respect from his captors, and they gave it to him.

Inform your captors of any health problems. If you need regular medicine or have other health problems, inform your captors as soon as possible. Similarly, should you subsequently develop any health problem in captivity, don't be reluctant to let them know about it. Hostages are a burden, and a healthy hostage is much easier to care for than a sick one. Moreover, a dead hostage is of little value. Thus, you will probably receive any medication or medical treatment you require.

Gather information about your captors. This will give you a sense of fighting back and may eventually pay dividends. While the kidnappers will probably hide their faces, you may be able to catch snatches of conversations. Try to learn their names, information about their families and their educational and class backgrounds, where they are from, and any life experiences that can be traced. Make mental notes about their physical characteristics, including height, weight, identifying marks (tattoos, scars, birthmarks), speech impediments, accents, or physical impairments. Leave fingerprints in out-of-the-way places in your cell. These can later prove that you were held captive there.

Fight stress and fear. If the normal tensions of your job cause sleep loss, then the tensions associated with captivity may turn you into an insomniac. Fear and forced inactivity may wreak havoc on your appetite. You may become more susceptible to sickness and suffer from headaches, weight loss, stomach problems, and a variety of other ailments. Establish a daily routine and stick to it as much as possible. Request soap, a toothbrush, and clean clothes. Try to make your life as normal as possible under the circumstances.

Escape

Generally, don't try to escape. More than likely you will fail and be subjected to harsh punishment. Your best chance of freedom and survival lies in your exchange for a ransom or your rescue by the authorities. Moreover, your captors generally will have considered all of the possible avenues of escape and have taken steps to ensure that they are not available to you.

Don't try to be heroic. During his captivity, Ambassador Asencio found that one of the terrorists had left his pistol on the back of the commode. Asencio didn't know whether it was a cruel joke, a test, or an opportunity. He knew that he was not skilled in the use of firearms, however, and that even if he was, the terrorists still outgunned him. While he might have been able to escape, he could just as easily have jeopardized the lives of the other hostages. Thus, he returned the gun to the terrorists. It was the right decision.

Consider escape only as a last resort. Only if you are positive that your captors are going to kill you should you attempt to escape. If, for example, they remove their hoods or your blindfold, it generally means that they no longer care whether you learn their identities and are planning to do away with you.

Successful escapes most often involve a great deal of preparation and thinking on your part. One kidnap victim who made a successful escape complained of intestinal problems each night and was permitted to go to the privy, near the edge of the jungle. As the routine continued, the sleepy guards became conditioned to his return and no longer accompanied him. Gradually, the prisoner spent more and more time in the privy, until one night he failed to return, having struck out for freedom.

Remember that storms and bad weather will mask your trail and make it more difficult for your captors to follow you. They will also make your escape more difficult.

10

Crisis Management

CORPORATE crisis management systems first evolved in the airline industry. Because of the magnitude of airline crashes and the intense public interest they generated, in the early years of commercial aviation a crash generally overwhelmed the management of the unfortunate airline. The airline had to deal with bereaved families, the press, safety investigators, public officials, the aircraft manufacturer, insurance companies, and lawsuits. Moreover, in the aftermath of a major crash, there was often a drop in ticket sales and the public had to be reassured about the safety of the airline.

To meet these challenges, the airlines gradually developed contingency plans that assigned specific roles and responsibilities to each senior corporate officer in the event of a crash. At many airlines, top officials were required to carry a copy of the contingency plan with them at all times. Over time, this planning paid off, and airlines today are able to manage periodic airline crashes with far more professionalism and responsiveness than in the past.

Crisis Management Team

Waiting for an emergency to arise before getting organized to deal with it is like shutting the barn door after the horse has already escaped. It's too late. Today you should try to anticipate crises before they occur and have mechanisms in place to deal with them in an organized, businesslike fashion. Failure to do so is likely to lead to disaster. One need only recall Union Carbide's mismanagement of the 1984 incident in Bhopal, India, to see how clumsily even a very large multinational company can behave if a well-thought-out crisis management plan is not in place. The Bhopal disaster is likely to cost Union Carbide stockholders hundreds of millions of dollars, if not more.

A corporate crisis management team (CMT) should be created before a problem arises. Select individuals who are cool-headed and experienced. If possible, all the individuals should reside in the same city and not be subject to extensive routine travel demands. Every member of the team should be required to fulfill the demands of the CMT personally and not delegate them to a subordinate. Alternates or deputy members also should be chosen in the event that one of the principal members is on vacation or indisposed when the crisis arises.

A chairman should be selected to preside over the team. You might consider hiring outside consultants to support the CMT and help implement decisions the team reaches. Clear lines of authority within the CMT should be established and individual responsibilities defined.

CMT representatives should have responsibility for each of the following functional categories:

- *Communications.* This individual coordinates all communications to and from the adversary, the host government (if the event takes place outside the United States), intermediaries, and law enforcement personnel to ensure that the company speaks with only one voice and does not send conflicting signals to any of the other parties involved.
- *Public relations.* This individual is the chief spokesman for the CMT and the liaison with the media. He or she should

answer all inquiries in a controlled and thoughtful manner in order to project a sense of strength and assurance. This person also will oversee efforts to repair negative publicity stemming from the crisis.

- *Legal.* The legal officer provides counsel to the CMT regarding the legal implications of the incident and the options being considered to resolve the situation. He or she will pay particular attention to the company's liability exposure.
- *Financial/insurance.* This person must judge the financial impact on the company and arrange for any funds necessary to implement the decisions of the CMT. In particular, he or she should establish contact with the firm's insurance company and attempt to anticipate the magnitude of the claims that can be expected because of the crisis.
- *Personnel.* The personnel officer provides support to and contact with the families of employees involved in the crisis. In a kidnapping situation, he or she also assembles all relevant medical data regarding the victim.
- *Security.* The security officer should play a major role in analyzing the threat, developing options, and implementing the CMT's decisions. He or she also should take steps to minimize the possibility of further attacks or incidents by invoking emergency security procedures at all company facilities.
- *Top management.* This individual acts as the representative of top management and the board of directors and keeps them informed of the deliberations and actions of the CMT.

Upon notification of a crisis, all members of the CMT should meet at a predesignated location. Notification may be by code word so as not to alarm others. Make certain that there is adequate secretarial and other staff support for the CMT. A secure communications system, copiers, telefax machines, and word processors should all be ready for the

CMT. You also might want to designate corporate aircraft and other assets to stand by in case the CMT needs them.

The CMT should have timely files and contingency plans to address all potential crises. In addition, all team members and their alternates should be required to stay abreast of political developments and terrorist activity in areas where your company operates. To this end, they should receive regular briefings (by outside experts if necessary), articles, and professional reports about relevant regions and countries.

Realistic training exercises should be implemented. The principle underlying all drills is to instill automatic responses in people. Thus, all members of the CMT should participate in regularly scheduled training exercises designed to be as realistic as possible. In addition to terrorist attacks, the team should be prepared for kidnappings, riots, technological failures, and natural disasters.

Kidnap Incidents

The following steps relate most directly to kidnapping incidents but also are applicable in addressing other crises.

Inform your employees of the risks. If you are sending employees to dangerous regions of the world, you have an obligation to inform them of the risks. If you do not, you and your company may be liable if some misfortune befalls them. The employee's decision to go must be based on a complete understanding of all of the possible risks.

If you provide security for your employees, make certain that it is good security. If your employees come to rely on the security you provide and something happens to one of them, then you and your company could be liable.

Provide your employees with instruction regarding living in and traveling to dangerous lands. The U.S. State Department and a number of other federal agencies provide such a course for their employees. Your attention to the welfare and safety of your employees may reduce your liability should any misfortune befall one of them, especially if the person disregarded the safety procedures contained in the course.

Be prepared to act immediately. If an employee is kidnapped or meets with some other misfortune, delay and indecision on your part could be grounds for litigation later.

Confirm the event. Don't do anything until you have verified the incident or threat. It may be a hoax or an erroneous report.

Don't expect the U.S. government to come to your rescue. The U.S. embassy can pressure the local government to take all possible measures to recover the kidnap victim and can provide intelligence and technology to local authorities, but it is unlikely to intervene in the internal affairs of another nation with respect to the kidnapping of a U.S. citizen. Thus, private citizens and U.S. multinationals generally have to rely on their own resources to resolve such crises.

Call the police. Most Western nations have effective law enforcement organizations. If the kidnappers contact you with a ransom demand, get in touch with the police immediately, despite threats by the kidnappers that they will take action against the hostage if you do. Generally, call the FBI in the United States, Scotland Yard in Great Britain, and the Royal Canadian Mounted Police in Canada. If the matter is not within their jurisdiction, they will assist you in reaching the proper authorities. Once the authorities are involved, they will develop a strategy for responding to the incident and will advise you accordingly.

Police in some Third World countries are far less organized and efficient when it comes to managing kidnapping incidents. In such cases, you and your company may have to manage the effort to recover the hostage. Be prepared to do so.

Send a representative to the scene. The field representative can be either an executive of the company or an outside contract employee. The presence of a person on the scene is clear evidence of corporate concern. The person you send should exhibit intelligence, maturity, good judgment, and effective communication skills. Don't send someone who is unfamiliar with the country and its language and customs. He or she could turn out to be an additional problem. The field representative should be in excellent health and be capable of spending days, perhaps even weeks or months, away from home, living under what may be difficult conditions. Should it be a protracted crisis, you may need a backup field representative or at least staff support to alleviate physical wear and tear on the primary representative.

Establish a chain of command. The field representative reports directly to the CMT and should not have the authority to make critical decisions without consultation, except when the victim's life is in imminent danger or when it is impossible to communicate with the CMT. The CMT should provide all necessary support to the field representative in an expeditious manner, and the CMT should be prepared to cut corporate red tape wherever and whenever necessary.

Establish a communications link. After arriving on the scene, the field representative should immediately establish a secure channel of communication with the CMT. If it is necessary to use open telephone or telex lines, which can be monitored easily, a preestablished code or cipher should be used to maintain the confidentiality of communications to and from the CMT. The most secure mode of communication is a portable scrambler phone that can be attached to any telephone. At the very least, it is wise to substitute innocuous words for key words such as ransom and the names of important local contacts. Similarly, the victim should never be identified by name. Different phrases can be used to indicate various options and courses of action.

Should your company have significant foreign operations, consider having a shortwave radio system installed at each plant or corporate office to be used in an emergency. During the Bhopal crisis, the Indian government shut down telephone and telex lines leading out of the stricken city, thus denying Union Carbide direct communication with its field representative. Union Carbide had not anticipated this possibility, and it allegedly handicapped their efforts to deal with the crisis.

Collect intelligence. The field representative should obtain all possible information regarding the kidnapping, including possible suspects or if the perpetrators are known, their identities, habits, modus operandi, and so forth. This information can be of critical importance. For example, some terrorist groups have a better history of smooth ransom exchanges than others. The field representative should make contact with local authorities and determine how much assistance they will provide in retrieving the victim. He or she also might want to make contact with local government and intelligence officials, as well as the U.S. embassy.

Ascertain the victim's medical requirements. If you suspect that the victim was injured in the abduction, his or her complete medical records should be available to facilitate treatment upon release. If life-sustaining drugs are required (insulin or medication for high blood pressure or a heart condition), it is prudent to stockpile a supply of the medication and try to communicate the victim's needs to the kidnappers at once. If the kidnap victim wears glasses, it is likely that these may have been lost or damaged in the abduction and subsequent captivity, thereby making it good policy to have a second pair on hand.

Establish and maintain contact with the kidnappers. Contact can be made in a variety of ways, but in most instances, the kidnappers will identify a specific channel of communication to be used for the duration of the negotiations, such as an ad in a newspaper or a particular individual. The field representative should have written proof of his identity and, if necessary, his authority to negotiate.

Protect and care for the victim's family. If the kidnapping occurs outside the United States and the victim's family is still in that country, appropriate security measures should be taken to prevent additional attacks on family members or related harassment. In most instances, it is wise to withdraw the victim's family from the host country. Religious, medical, and psychological counseling should be made available to family members, but only at their request. The family should be kept informed of any developments as they relate to efforts to secure the victim's release. Be prepared to assist the family with its financial obligations, especially in cases where the wife is not knowledgeable about the family finances. Other support groups, some run by the relatives of former victims, can be very effective in helping the families of kidnap victims weather the crisis. Efforts also should be made to shield family members from what is often callous and inconsiderate media attention.

Be prepared to experience family resentment directed at you, other corporate officers, and the company itself. Until their loved one is freed, they may blame you. You are likely to be accused of slackness and of not doing enough, for you will be playing a waiting game and will not always appear to be working to free the victim. Try to understand the family's need to vent their anger about the situation.

Formulate a negotiating plan. The CMT should formulate a detailed negotiating plan based on information collected by the field representative and provided by other sources. The plan should include an assessment of the elasticity of the ransom demands, focusing on the minimum and maximum estimates of a negotiated ransom payment and detailing the steps by which the ransom will be paid. If you are not insured, assemble a ransom fund as soon as possible so that you will not have to frantically liquidate assets or raid bank accounts at the last minute. An analysis of previous kidnappings has shown that the lack of a firm negotiating plan was a significant handicap in achieving the release of kidnap victims. A sound, comprehensive negotiating plan represents a team approach and permits a wide variety of perspectives and different kinds of knowledge to be factored into the decision-making process.

Work on public relations. Public relations will be important both before and after the incident. Much of your public relations task should already have been accomplished before the crisis. If your company has a positive image in the country where the incident occurred, it may greatly assist your efforts to recover your employee.

In addition to keeping tight control on information being released to the public, you also will have to decide what to tell your other employees.

Promote good relations with the media. If you regard the media as the enemy, you will only compound your problems. Your antagonism will simply engender their hostility. It is extremely difficult to keep a major kidnapping or similar incident under wraps, so don't try. Instead, make an effort to manage the flow of information in a way that will not be detrimental to the hostage or ongoing negotiations for his return. At the same time, disseminate pertinent facts about the episode with a minimum of editorializing or embellishment.

The performance of Johnson & Johnson, especially its chairman, in the aftermath of the Tylenol poisonings is a good example of how to handle a major corporate crisis. In the final analysis, the public may have a right to know, but you, your company, the hostage, and his family all have rights as well.

Whatever you do, don't concede the battle to the media and allow them to portray the incident in whatever fashion they see fit. If this happens, you may lose both public support and the cooperation of local authorities. Your goal should be to humanize the issues surrounding the incident as much as possible. Portray the victim not as an American or as a representative of your company, but as a loving father/mother, husband/wife, son/daughter, brother/sister deserving of sympathy.

In addition, remember that terrorism is nothing without media coverage. Indeed, the goal of most terrorists is to kill or kidnap one person and intimidate millions. Media coverage of terrorist acts might not only interfere in resolving the incident, but also encourages copycat crimes by other criminals or terrorists. Detailed media coverage of an incident may provide a primer for other groups learning the trade.

Be aware of local laws. The legal representative of the CMT is responsible for reviewing all local laws, customs, and regulations impinging on kidnapping cases. Certain countries have laws that may affect a corporation's continued presence and activities there after a kidnapping. For example, some countries forbid negotiating with terrorists or giving publicity to terrorist groups, while others prohibit the paying of ransoms. If domestic laws are broken in the process of ransoming or retrieving a kidnap victim, the company may have to bear the consequences.

According to a recent study, the following countries prohibit the payment of ransoms or attach criminal penalties to those who do: Chile, Colombia, Cyprus, Ghana, Guatemala, Italy, Qatar, Singapore, Trinidad and Tobago, and Yugoslavia.

While such laws may be on the books, enforcement varies from country to country.

During the 1970s the release of hostage William F. Niehous was made far more difficult by Venezuelan laws prohibiting his employer, Owens-Illinois, from negotiating with kidnappers or complying with their demands. While laws of this kind ultimately may deny support and sustenance to terrorist organizations, it is often at the sacrifice of the kidnap victim. This is, of course, completely unacceptable to the friends, relatives, and employers of the victim. In such situations, negotiations for the release of the captive often must be moved to a third country and cloaked in secrecy.

Consider kidnap and ransom insurance. There was a tremendous growth in kidnap and ransom (K&R) insurance during the 1970s and 1980s, but this reportedly leveled off in the late 1980s. First offered in 1938 by Lloyd's of London, which reportedly still controls the largest share of the market, a number of American underwriters now provide the same kind of protection. With increased competition, premiums have decreased. Today, K&R insurance generally is a very good buy and should be investigated by all companies and individuals desiring peace of mind. Premium rates typically are figured on the basis of considerations such as the country in question, the number of people covered, the level of the threat against them, security precautions in place, travel patterns, and the amount of the deductible.

The existence of a K&R policy should be kept a closely guarded secret because knowledge that a substantial policy is in force may serve as an incentive to terrorists to kidnap the policyholder, since they may reckon that payment of the ransom will be sure and swift. A second problem with kidnap insurance is that not all insurance companies pay automatically and some will attempt to negotiate the ransom downward, a process that could take several months or longer.

There is a movement afoot in Great Britain to outlaw K&R insurance. It has been alleged that the existence of such insurance encourages kidnappings and is an important source of financing for terrorist groups.

Verify the hostage's safety. In several cases, terrorists have botched kidnappings, killing or mortally wounding the intended subject. The terrorists kept the body and proceeded to negotiate for the ransom as if the victim was still alive. Before any negotiation takes place, the negotiator or field representative must demand and receive proof that the victim is still alive and in good health and demand that such verification be provided by the kidnappers on a continuous basis. The receipt of personal articles belonging to the victim does not constitute satisfactory verification since it establishes only that the victim was at some time in the hands of the terrorists and provides no assurance as to his or her welfare. Similarly, letters from the victim can be forged or postdated and therefore are unacceptable. Direct communication by telephone from the victim to someone who knows him or her extremely well is the best method of verification, but photographs of the victim holding the front page of a major daily newspaper with the headline clearly legible also will suffice. If tape recordings of the victim are used, the victim must describe recent athletic scores or news items so that the tape can be time locked; otherwise, it will not constitute adequate verification. The failure to press for continuous verification of the victim's well-being may suggest that the terrorists can kill him or her and still collect the ransom.

Maintain the field representative's security. Terrorists are capable of any treachery. In several instances, the field representative or negotiator was taken prisoner by the kidnappers and held for ransom along with the original victim. Thus, the field representative must take steps to ensure his own security and to prevent the hijacking or interception of the ransom once it is in his possession. Precautions may include a secure dwelling, bodyguards, a hardened automobile, and body armor. The field representative should not take unnecessary risks. Thus, meetings and exchanges should be conducted only in areas where both the field representative and the kidnappers feel secure.

Negotiate the ransom. Terrorists normally demand some kind of ransom in exchange for the kidnap victim. Most often the ransom will take the form of money, although sometimes it will involve the release of prisoners (U.S. hostages in Lebanon), the free distribution of food to the poor (Argentina), and even salary increases and bonuses for workers in a particular plant or factory (Colombia). You can negotiate with nearly all kidnappers; few actually desire the death of their hostage and prefer instead to realize their ransom demands, if only in part.

All negotiations take time and should not be rushed unless there is genuine concern for the hostage's well-being. If the ransom demand is paid too rapidly, the kidnappers may conclude that they asked too little. This occurred during an incident in Central America, and the kidnappers tripled the ransom.

Once an understanding has been reached concerning the amount of the ransom, a delivery schedule and procedures to implement the delivery also must be agreed on. It is always preferable if the kidnap victim and ransom can be exchanged simultaneously. The dropping of the ransom payment at a predesignated location in return for a promise that the victim will be released later involves trusting the terrorists to perform their part of the bargain. This author recommends that you never trust terrorists or kidnappers.

Money is both bulky and heavy in large amounts and requires the carrier to have a good deal of strength and stamina. One million dollars in $50 bills, for example, weighs 40.8 pounds and fills a large suitcase. Usually, however, kidnappers will demand nonserialized $10 and $20 bills, which are easier to circulate without attracting attention. It takes fifty thousand $20 bills, weighing 102.5 pounds, to make a ransom of $1 million (there are 490 new bank notes of any denomination to a pound).

If you are working with the authorities, they may want to chemically treat the bills so that traces of the chemical will later be visible on the kidnappers' hands. Similarly, a hidden transmitter might be built into the container holding the money. Sophisticated kidnappers are familiar with most money identification techniques and will often repack the money in their own suitcases or bags to guard against the latter ruse. Moreover, should they discover that they have been double-crossed, the ransom is sure to be increased and the hostage's life may be placed in even more danger.

Negotiating style. Conventional wisdom is to negotiate until negotiation fails to get results or the hostage's life appears to be in imminent danger. Contrary to what you may think, time is on your side. Not only does the passage of time increase the risk that the authorities may discover the hideout of the kidnappers and rescue the hostage, but the kidnappers may grow weary of the tension and demands involved in holding a hostage. In addition, the kidnappers may start to form a bond with their captive, and this bond may contribute to their desire to get the unpleasantness over with.

The field representative or negotiator should make it clear from the outset that he does not have the authority to make binding agreements (even if this isn't true) and must confer with the CMT before committing the company to any specific course of action. This should reduce the pressure on the field representative and prevent him from being boxed into a corner when negotiating.

When negotiating with terrorists, always be unemotional, straightforward, and businesslike. Never lie to them about the terms and conditions of an agreement and, to the degree possible, skirt potentially volatile issues. Establish the image of a cooperative individual who is trying to resolve the incident to everyone's satisfaction. Never provide a flat "no" to any terrorist demand that might provoke an outburst of rage that could have tragic consequences. Never call the terrorist's bluff. Always strive to give the impression that progress is being made.

Always start your negotiations by naming a sum of money (if that is the issue) that is much lower than that demanded by the kidnappers. At the same time, do not start so low as to offend the kidnappers, causing them to break off negotiations altogether. Bargain for everything; don't give the kidnappers anything for free. There should be a cost attached to any concession, no matter how small. Any request made by the kidnappers should be met with a counter-request.

If their demands are totally unreasonable or beyond your company's power to satisfy, consider employing the "good guy, bad guy" routine. Have a co-negotiator break the bad news to them so that you can maintain your position as reasonable and reassuring. With luck, the kidnappers will continue to talk to you.

Be prepared for the hostage to turn against you. Captivity and powerlessness may have a profound impact on the hostage. He may come to resent the negotiator (and the company) for trying to bargain the terrorists down and drawing out his captivity. He may come to fear a police assault, which could put his life in jeopardy. He may begin to suffer from the Stockholm syndrome, described in chapter 9. Some employees have sued their employers, maintaining that not enough was done to secure their release or that the negotiations were drawn out far too long.

Upon release of the hostage, have someone on the scene to provide comfort. Psychologists have observed that victims often undergo a second state of panic after they are released. Even after the danger is over, it will be necessary to reestablish an emotional support system for the victim. Generally, rescue personnel will be too concerned with other matters to be much help. Have a close friend of the victim or a psychologist on hand to greet the hostage.

Provide for postcrisis psychological problems. The hostage may be tormented by feelings that he did not do enough to resist and in fact acted as a collaborator. He may feel guilty that he caused so much concern and so many problems for his family and friends. He may worry that he was brainwashed. Some former hostages have difficulty adjusting to life after their ordeal; things that once seemed important no longer mean as much.

Give the victim an opportunity to vent his feelings. Let him know that such feelings are common among former hostages and are nothing to be ashamed or embarrassed about. Provide him with reassurance and understanding. Let the former hostage blend back into the company at his own pace.

Mount a rescue operation only as a last resort. If it is impossible to comply with the terrorists' ransom demands—for example, if they adamantly refuse to release the victim unless certain political prisoners are freed from jail and the government refuses to comply—it may be necessary to mount a private sector rescue operation. To do so one must enter the world of highly specialized firms with extraordinary political, military, and intelligence capabilities and a willingness to undertake extremely difficult tasks for a sum of money commensurate with the risk involved. Although many self-styled mercenaries may indicate a desire to attempt such a mission, most will spend a good deal of your money without producing any results. Moreover, should they actually mount a rescue effort, they are likely to get both themselves and the hostage killed. There is no room for amateurs in this field. Several of the large insurance underwriters are affiliated with firms skilled in hostage negotiation and retrieval, and you should consider retaining one of them.

Remember that rescue efforts may violate any number of national statutes and involve a good deal of risk for those involved. Moreover, mounting such an effort is likely to have serious consequences for your company and its future operations in the country whose territory is violated. Such an effort should be considered only when all else fails.

Prepare a postincident report. At the conclusion of the terrorist incident, you should prepare a postincident report so that deficiencies can be identified and corrected before another incident occurs. The report also enables you to share what you have learned with others. In the final analysis, knowledge is perhaps the most valuable defense against kidnapping and other forms of terrorism.

11

Firearms, Body Armor, and Electronic Countermeasures

Some of you probably skipped ahead to this chapter. Hands trembling in anticipation, you are waiting for me to describe the finer points of blasting holes in your adversary using the latest space-age gadgetry. Unfortunately, I am going to disappoint you. Shops that cater to the would-be James Bond generally are selling fantasies, not real protection. Gadgetry and firearms play, at best, a small role in defending yourself. There are some things, however, that you should know about equipment and firearms available for personal protection.

Firearms

Don't try to shoot it out with "Carlos." I cannot stress this enough. If you are ambushed, your primary goal should be to remove yourself from danger as quickly as possible. Forget about heroics; trust in God and Adidas and get the hell out of there.

Your adversary will almost always have the firepower advantage. The terrorists, and there will probably be several, most often will be armed with automatic weapons, usually assault rifles or submachine guns. Sometimes they also will have grenades and rockets. Your pistol may be fine for making the neighborhood thug practice his metier elsewhere, but a terrorist is not some punk with a sharpened screwdriver. Against heavily armed and well-trained terrorists, who also have the advantage of surprise and concealment, you do not stand much of a chance armed solely with a small-caliber handgun.

You can only do so many things at once. Your chief objective, as stated earlier, should be to escape. If you try to put up resistance at the same time, you are likely to do both things badly and therefore reduce your chances of survival.

If you shoot back, you may start a firefight. Any armed resistance not only will distract you from what should be your primary objective (that is, to escape), but it may enrage the terrorists or cause them to fire back indiscriminately, believing that their own lives are in jeopardy. Remember, you are the object of a kidnapping attempt, and the terrorists want you undamaged if at all possible.

Guns are not for impressing people. Take a good, long look at yourself. If you are considering buying a gun for self-defense, make sure your motive is not to play John Wayne. Guns are serious business and require a good deal of discipline and training to be used in a safe and prudent manner. They are not an extension of your manhood or for flashing in bars. If you have a tendency to drink too much, if your temper has a low flash point, or if you have small children around the house, then rethink any notion of acquiring a gun. It may ultimately give you more grief than safety.

Investigate the local statutes relating to gun ownership. Some urban jurisdictions prohibit handgun ownership altogether. Most firearms appropriate to this discussion require some kind of license, as does carrying a concealed weapon. I do not recommend that you acquire a firearm in violation of local ordinances. Note that many foreign countries have even tougher firearms laws than the United States, especially countries in Western Europe.

There are some instances in which you and your bodyguards should consider carrying weapons. Such situations generally involve a very high threat level. In countries where there is a great deal of civil strife or terrorist activity, it may be prudent to be armed at all times. In such instances, take some common sense precautions.

Not all guns are self-protection weapons. An assault rifle is the weapon of choice for an infantryman, but it can be unwieldy inside a vehicle. If it is set on automatic or burst mode, it may be too indiscriminate for you to use in a crowded area. Moreover, it is often too powerful to be used inside a house or office, since its high-velocity bullets can travel through walls and could injure other members of your family or staff. Finally, an assault rifle is not convenient to carry around, and a gun that is not there when you need it is no protection at all.

Submachine guns are more portable (many models fit easily in a briefcase) and have a high rate of fire. They are not terribly accurate, however, especially in full-auto mode, and have a tendency to climb. Some models also jam frequently and therefore suffer in the reliability category. The most serious problem regarding submachine guns is that they are illegal (without a proper license) in the United States and Western Europe.

You may want a shotgun. A shotgun is simple to operate, and little can malfunction or jam on nonautomatic models. Whether you are using buckshot or solid slugs, a shotgun puts out devastating fire at close range. Moreover, shotguns are legal almost everywhere. The policeman who would do a double take on seeing your Uzi would not look twice at a shotgun on the wall.

Because a shotgun fires a salvo of projectiles rather than just one, it is a more effective weapon for someone who does not have time to practice frequently. Point the shotgun in the right direction, pull the trigger, and you are likely to hit something. Even if you don't, shotguns are extremely intimidating when you are on the receiving end of one.

Shotguns are safer than handguns. If you are going to have a gun around the house, shotguns are more difficult for a child to manipulate than a loaded pistol. Thus, the odds of an accidental discharge are reduced. In addition, when fired in close quarters, buckshot is far less likely to pass through walls than high-velocity bullets.

What is the most effective shotgun? A short-barrel pump riot shotgun is probably the most effective model for self-defense. Check with your local police to learn what the minimum length of the barrel must be.

If you have a handgun, make certain that you know how to use it. Without constant practice, even the best pistol shots get rusty. Don't expect that a few hours on the range every six months will be enough to ensure that you can use your weapon competently in a pinch. Consider taking a course on combat handgun techniques with a qualified instructor. Work with him to find a stance and a grip that are comfortable and effective. Ask him to help you sight your weapon in. Know your weapon: how to strip it, clear it when it jams, and care for it. Work with a qualified instructor or your security chief to select the right handgun for your purposes.

Body Armor

The classic bulletproof vest. First, the term *bulletproof* is misleading. There is no such thing as a bulletproof garment. Some garments will prevent some bullets from passing through or will reduce the impact and damage caused by a bullet, but no garment will make you impervious to all projectiles, whatever their velocity, caliber, and composition. Bullets with superhard points or coated with Teflon will defeat virtually any garment without added reinforcement on the market today.

What is body armor? Protective garments come in all shapes and sizes, from vests to raincoats, blazers, and even lingerie. Nancy Reagan, for example, had a slip that was designed to be a piece of body armor.

Most protective garments are made of woven synthetic fibers that stop a bullet by dissipating the force of the impact, like a ball hitting a net. Protective garments are constructed to provide different levels of protection, and some garments even permit you to add more armor to custom fit your situation. Indeed, flak vests (generally used by the military) often have pieces of steel inserted in various pockets to increase the level of protection. The more protection your garment offers, the heavier and bulkier it is likely to be. Select your protective garment to meet the highest level of threat you expect to face. Note: A heavy, bulky garment may be obvious to a potential attacker and cause him to aim for your head or to use a more powerful weapon.

While your protective garment may stop a bullet, it may not defeat a knife. The woven fabric of most garments is vulnerable to forceful knife thrusts.

If you are shot while wearing a protective garment, don't expect to come away totally unscathed. A bullet to the chest is still going to pack a wallop. Even if your protective garment prevents it from penetrating your flesh, be prepared for a nasty bruise and perhaps even broken ribs. Depending on your size and strength, the impact of even a medium-caliber slug can knock you off your feet.

Make certain that your protective garments are comfortable. If they are uncomfortable, you won't wear them and they won't provide you with any protection.

Take good care of your protective garments. Inferior cleaning techniques, too much exposure to the sun, and excessive wear all take their toll. With time and poor care, protective garments will lose some of their ability to stop a bullet.

Don't be taken in by some of the products on the market. Ballistic cloth caps will not provide you with real protection from head shots; the impact of the bullet alone will probably shatter your skull. Nothing short of a helmet will offer your head any real protection.

Electronic Countermeasures

Is there anything you can do to discover whether your phone line is tapped? Forget about ads for devices that claim to alert you if your telephone line is tapped. Most of them don't work at all, and the rest are effective only against the most obvious and unsophisticated wiretaps. Such devices merely detect voltage variations in the line, not a competently installed bug. To be reasonably certain that your lines are clean, you need the services of a reputable professional with highly sophisticated equipment. The process is expensive and time-consuming, and there is no absolute assurance that your adversary isn't more sophisticated than the person you hired to take electronic countermeasures. As one recent internal government report concluded, "No countermeasures equipment was found which could conclusively determine the existence of a properly installed wiretap." Nevertheless, it is still a good idea to sweep your telephones and lines on a regular basis.

Sweeping your phones requires sophisticated equipment. To test your telephone, the technician will run an electrical current or sound through each component to activate the bug. For this, he will use a telephone analyzer. To the extent possible, he will have to trace your telephone line back to the phone company's central office, noting and accounting for each connection that has been hooked to it. For this, he will need a time domain reflectometer. This will provide him with a picture of what your telephone wire looks like electronically. He will then compare this picture with one of a clean telephone line.

Be aware of other communications vulnerabilities. While your phones may be clean, your telex and telefax machines may not be. Have them checked as well.

Purchase scramblers. As noted in chapter 5, the most reliable and effective means of improving your telephone security is to purchase portable scrambler devices. The only scramblers that work, however, are those that fit your telephone and the telephones of all the people with whom you may want to speak. To anyone listening, scrambled conversations are unintelligible, and it will take time and sophisticated computers to reconstruct an intercepted conversation. Remember that your conversations can still be compromised by other bugs in the room you are calling from (or to) or by a bug in the scrambler itself.

Be discreet when talking on the telephone. Even if you employ appropriate safeguards, it is wise not to say anything on the telephone that you would not say to the competition, a grand jury, or your spouse. Also do not discuss travel plans or security arrangements over the telephone.

Use babble tapes or background music to mask your conversation. Your security officer can make such a babble tape by recording the din at a local tavern or restaurant. Music also can be used to make it harder to distinguish your voice from the background noise. Any kind of constant background noise will help prevent eavesdropping by an adversary who bounces a laser beam off your window and uses a computer to convert the vibrations into sound.

Counter eavesdropping devices when traveling. In addition to carrying a portable scrambler, you can use two other devices to provide minimal protection. A field-strength detector will identify a magnetic field created by a transmitter implanted in a wall or your furniture. A feedback detector sends out its own signal, which will be transmitted back through the bug. The former sells for around $600 and the latter for approximately $800. Neither will protect you from all microphones.

Sweeping rooms is costly and time-consuming. Many debugging companies are not honest enough to give you a realistic appraisal of what a thorough search will cost. There are so many places in the average room where a listening device can be hidden and so many varieties of listening devices that a real search will take a good deal of time and money. In a truly thorough search, the furniture will be x-rayed and the walls examined inch by inch. Using a nonlinear junction detector, which emits a signal revealing the presence of a microphone's electronic components in the wall, a competent technician can find most microphones. Every wire in the room also must be examined by a technician with a telephone repairman's handset to see if it is carrying a voice signal. You can never be absolutely certain, however, that the room is clean.

Realizing that most clients will not spring for the kind of money required to undertake a comprehensive search, unscrupulous firms often conduct superficial searches and then report that everything is all right. If a listening device turns up in a subsequent search, they will suggest that it must have been planted later.

Find a reputable company to do your sweeps and pay the company what it is worth. If its appraisal is more than you want to pay, consider having the company sweep only certain key offices and phone lines.

A Final Word

Beware of technological fetishism. While technology will always be important, avoid depending too heavily on it for your protection. In the final analysis, reliable security will remain chiefly the product of hard work, good planning, and common sense.

Appendix
Checklists

Emergency Data: Personal Checklist

1. Name ____________________
2. Other name/alias ____________________
3. Age ____________________
4. Place of birth ____________________
5. Sex ____________________
6. Race ____________________
7. Weight ____________________
8. Height ____________________
9. Glasses/prescription ____________________
   ____
10. Identifying marks/characteristics ____________________
    ____
    ____
11. Addresses
    Home ____________________
    Office ____________________
12. Phone numbers
    Home ____________________
    Office ____________________
    Car ____________________
    Other ____________________
    Listed or unlisted? ____________________
13. Social Security number ____________________
14. Credit cards/numbers ____________________
    ____
15. Physicians/dentists ____________________
    ____
    ____
    ____

16. Health
    General condition ______
    Problems ______
    ______
    Blood type ______
    Medication(s) ______
    Allergies ______
17. Spouse ______
18. Children (names and ages) ______
    ______
    ______
19. Schools attended by children ______
    ______
    ______
20. Name(s) of contact(s) at school(s) ______
    ______
    ______
21. Vehicles and license numbers ______
    ______
    ______
22. Plane (type and description) ______
    ______
23. Boat (type and description) ______
    ______
24. Client's special skills
    Driver's license (state, number, expiration date) ______
    ______
    Pilot's license (type, number, etc.) ______
    ______
    Foreign languages ______
    Professional background ______
    ______
    ______
    Military service ______
    Survival skills/terrorism awareness courses ______
    ______

Aggressive/evasive driving courses ______________

____

Security clearance ______________________

25. Firearms

Does client own a firearm? ______________

Type and caliber ______________________

Does client carry a firearm? ______________

Does client have firearms training? ____________

____

26. Name of client's secretary/personal assistant ________

____

Address and phone number ______________

____

27. Name of client's attorney ______________

____

Address and phone number ______________

____

28. Does client have kidnap and ransom insurance? _____

____

Policy, agent, and underwriter ______________

____

____

29. Name, address, and phone number of client's bank __

____

____

Contact ______________________________

30. Name of client's chief of security ______________

Address and phone number ______________

31. History of threats against client and family ________

____

____

____

____

32. Any known enemies? ______________________

____

33. Regular places client visits (address and phone number)

____

____

____

____

____

34. Client should provide the following:
    a. fingerprints
    b. blueprints of all residences
    c. handwriting sample
    d. photograph
    e. voice tape

Country Risk: Background Information for Executives Traveling Abroad

1. Name of country ______________________
2. Population ______________________
3. Racial/ethnic characteristics ______________________

   ____
4. Religion ______________________
5. Climate ______________________
6. Capital ______________________
7. Gross national product (GNP) ______________________
8. Chief exports ______________________
9. Type of government ______________________
10. Name of head of state ______________________
11. Major allies ______________________
12. Name of currency and current conversion rate ______

    ____
13. Is a visa required to enter country? ______________________
14. What vaccinations are required? ______________________

    ____
15. Special medications that should be taken ______________

    ____

    ____
16. Health

    Water (avoid?) ______________________

    Foods to avoid ______________________

    Insects ______________________

    General hygiene ______________________
17. Violence or instability index ______________________

    ____

    ____

18. Major terrorist groups operating in country ________
____
____

19. Evaluation of street crime ________________
____
____

20. Evaluation of local police and military ________
____
____

21. Special hazards ________________________
____
____

22. Local customs
    Dos ________________________________
    ____
    ____

    Don'ts ______________________________
    ____
    ____

23. List of helpful terms in local language
    Police ______________________________
    Help _______________________________
    Thank you ___________________________
    Hello ______________________________
    Please ______________________________
    Excuse me __________________________
    Bathroom ___________________________
    Other ______________________________

24. Bribes and gratuities
    How common? _______________________
    Where needed? ______________________
    General advice ______________________
    ____
    ____

Hotels: Security Checklist

1. Name of hotel ______________________________
2. Address ______________________________
3. Phone ______________________________
4. Date of visit ______________________________
5. List of clients and guests who will be staying at the hotel
   ____
   ____
   ____
6. Name of hotel manager ______________________________
   Assistant manager ______________________________
   Phone extension ______________________________
7. Name of security director ______________________________
   Assistant security director ______________________________
   Phone extension ______________________________
8. Hotel staff
   Doorman ______________________________
   Bell captain ______________________________
   Maid(s) assigned to room ______________________________
   ____
   Hotel doctor ______________________________
   Valet ______________________________
   Secretarial services ______________________________
9. Reservations confirmed by ______________________________
   Confirmation number ______________________________
   Who made reservations? ______________________________
   Method of payment ______________________________
   Safe deposit box ______________________________
   Description of room(s) ______________________________
   How will client arrive and depart? ______________________________
   ____

10. Arrival
    Date ____________________
    Approximate time ____________________
    Airport ____________________
    Flight number and airline ____________________
    Time of flight ____________________
    Other means of transport ____________________
    Car or limo service ____________________
    Helicopter service ____________________
11. Departure
    Date ____________________
    Approximate time ____________________
    Airport ____________________
    Flight number and airline ____________________
    Time of flight ____________________
    Other means of transport ____________________
    Car or limo service ____________________
    Helicopter service ____________________
12. General comments about hotel ____________________
    ____
    ____
    ____

    Location: area of city/street activity/congestion
    ____
    ____
    ____

    Nearest police station ____________________
    ____

    Nearest hospital ____________________
    Nearest fire station ____________________
    Elevators: number/location/condition ____________________
    ____

    Stairways/stairwells ____________________
    ____

    Fire extinguishers ____________________
    Smoke detectors ____________________

13. Communications
    Switchboard/security
    Telex: number/security
    Fax machine: number/security
    Mail/deliveries
    Photocopier
14. Hotel services
    Beauty parlor/barbershop
    Newsstand
    Spa/gym
    Cocktail lounge(s): location/security
    Pool
    Pets
    Nearest jogging area
15. Restaurant(s)/dining
    Location
    Hours of operation
    Cuisine
    Dress code
    Choice of table(s)
    Special dietary requirements
    Name of maître d'
    Names of captain/waiter(s)
    General security

Restaurant(s)/dining (continued)

Deficiencies ______________________________

____

Room service ______________________________

16. Room survey

Number(s) ______________________________

Location ______________________________

Survey of rooms on either side, across the hall ____

____

____

Nearest fire exit/directions ______________________________

____

Alternate exit ______________________________

Smoke detector ______________________________

Door lock(s) ______________________________

Sprinkler system ______________________________

Balcony ______________________________

Ledge ______________________________

Windows ______________________________

Telephone(s)/extension number(s) ______________________________

____

____

Deficiencies ______________________________

____

____

17. Room numbers of those accompanying client

Security detail ______________________________

____

Other family members ______________________________

____

Other staff ______________________________

____

18. Perimeter security/outside doors and exits ____________

____

____

Are all doors/exits manned? ______________________________

Are doors locked late at night? ________________
Is there closed-circuit television? ________________
Grounds ________________________________
____

19. Security staff
General attitude ________________________________
____
Training/professionalism ________________________
____
Are staff members armed? ________________________

20. Garage/parking
Security evaluation ______________________________
____
Special arrangements ____________________________
____

21. Recent crimes at hotel/vicinity (check with local police) ________________________________
____
____

22. Special services required by client ________________
____
____
____

23. Entertainment outside hotel
Restaurants ________________________________
____
____
Nightclubs ________________________________
____
____
Theaters ________________________________
____
____
Other ________________________________
____
____

24. Overall evaluation of hotel and its security ________
____
____
____
____

Building Survey: Security Checklist

1. Name and address of building

____

____

____

____

2. Name and phone number of manager/superintendent

____

____

3. Directions to building ______________________

____

____

____

4. Type of building/construction _______________

____

5. Number of floors ____________________________
6. Number of entrances/exits ___________________
7. Type of roof ________________________________
8. Number of workers ___________________________
9. List of tenants _____________________________

____

____

____

____

____

____

____

____

10. Type of windows _____________________________
11. Do windows open? ____________________________

12. Fire escape? ______________________
    Ladder? ______________________
13. Sprinkler system? ______________________
14. Security forces
    Name of company/service ______________________
    Contact ______________________
    Phone number ______________________
    Address ______________________
    Uniformed guards? ______________________
    Training ______________________
    Armed? ______________________
    Twenty-four hours a day? ______________________
    Patrols? ______________________
    On-site telephone? ______________________
15. Type of access control ______________________
    ____
    ____
    Closed-circuit television? ______________________
    Location of monitors ______________________
    Are monitors always manned? ______________________
    Is building open to public? ______________________
    During the day __________ At night __________
    I.D. badges required? ______________________
    Type ______________________
16. Garage/parking
    Location ______________________
    Access control? ______________________
    Patrolled? ______________________
    Spaces marked? ______________________
17. Client's office space
    Suite number and location ______________________
    ____
    Locks and security ______________________
    ____
    File cabinets (locked?) ______________________
    Mail screening? ______________________

Panic button? ____________________

Shredder(s)? ____________________

Office security procedures? ____________________

____

____

Security manual? ____________________

18. Deficiencies ____________________

____

____

____

____

____

Residential Security: Checklist

General Information

1. Name of client ____________________
2. Address of residence ____________________
 ____
3. Directions to reach residence ____________________
 ____
4. Telephone number(s) ____________________
5. Names of all family members living at residence ______
 ____
 ____
 ____
 ____
6. Names of all members of household staff and description of their duties ____________________
 ____
 ____
 ____
7. Names and duties of all other employees and regular service personnel ____________________
 ____
 ____
 ____
8. Make, model, and license numbers of all cars regularly at residence ____________________
 ____
9. History of previous break-ins and security problems
 ____
 ____
 ____

Exterior

1. Is there a gate? ______
2. Is the gate solid and in good repair? ______
3. Is it manned? ______ Hours ______
4. Is there a closed-circuit television camera on the gate? ______
5. Is the gate locked? ______ During the day? ______ At night? ______
6. Is there a fence or wall surrounding the house? ______
   Type and construction ______
   Sensors? ______
   Deficiencies ______
7. Have all poles, trees, and sheds that might help an intruder scale the wall/fence been eliminated? ______
   Deficiencies ______
8. Is there an exterior lighting system? ______
   Type and location ______
   Deficiencies ______
9. Are lights checked regularly to see that they are working? ______
10. How good are outside doors? ______
11. How good are locks on outside doors? ______
    Are locks firmly mounted? ______
    Are locks in good working order? ______
12. Are all hinges firmly mounted? ______
    Are exterior hinges protected against removal? ______
    ______
13. Can any doors be penetrated by breaking glass or light wood panel? ______
14. Are doors equipped with vertical dead bolt secondary locks? ______
15. Are all keys to exterior doors accounted for? ______
    Names of all who have keys ______
    ______
    ______

16. Can all windows, balcony doors, and sliding doors be securely locked? ______
    Deficiencies ______
17. Are all doors equipped with a peephole? ______
18. Are all external buildings locked? ______
19. Are there trees and poles that might give an intruder easy access to the upper floors? ______
    Are all ladders secured and trellises removed? ______
20. Are there external hazards that should be corrected?
    ______
21. Can the garage be locked? ______
    Are the locks in good working order? ______
22. Are there places (ditches, heavy brush, or trees) where a sniper could hide? ______
23. Are all of the windows of the house protected by shutters, iron bars, or an effective alarm system? ______
    ______
24. Are all windows kept locked when they are closed?
    ______
25. Are basement windows effectively secured? ______
26. Are windows hardened, or fitted with bullet-resistant glass? ______
27. If there are sliding glass doors, are there bars in the track to prevent them from being forced? ______
28. Is there trash or refuse on the property that could harbor dangerous insects or be used to hide a bomb? ______
29. Is the garbage properly secured (or shredded) to ensure that outsiders cannot browse through it for information about the family? ______
30. Is the mailbox secure? ______
31. Does the house have a backup electrical generator? ______
    Location ______
32. What kind of response force is there in the event of an intruder or other emergency? ______
    ______

33. Is a guard force maintained? ______
    Number of guards ______
    Location of guards ______
    Is there a central station? ______
    Are guards armed? ______
    What are their rules of engagement? ______
    ______
    What training have guards received? ______
    ______
    Do the guards patrol the property? ______

Interior

1. Does the house have an alarm system? ______
    Type and model ______
    Is it well installed and maintained? ______
    Are there redundancies built into the system? ______
2. Do family members and servants have proper training to identify letter/parcel bombs? ______
3. Do family members and servants require all guests to identify themselves before admitting them? ______
4. Do family members and servants know what to do in an emergency? ______
5. Is there a safe room in the house? ______
    Location ______
    Special features and equipment ______
    ______
6. Is every member of the household staff screened? ______
7. Are all skylights, roof hatches, and roof doors properly secured? ______
8. Does the house have smoke detectors? ______
9. Does the house have an adequate number of fire extinguishers? ______
    Are they filled and in good working order? ______
    Do all members of the household know how to use them? ______

10. Is there an inventory of all valuable property? ______
11. Are emergency numbers posted by all telephones? ___
12. Have steps been taken to secure telephones? ________
13. Have household personnel been provided with security awareness training? ____________________
    If so, what kind? ____________________
14. Do all members of the household staff know how to spot surveillance? ____________________
15. Household hazards and security deficiencies ________
    ____
    ____
    ____
    ____

Selected Bibliography

Alexander, Yonah, and Robert A. Kilmarx, eds. *Political Terrorism and Business*. New York: Praeger, 1979.

Ashwood, Capt. Thomas M. *Terror in the Skies*. New York: Stein and Day, 1987.

Bolz, Captain Frank A. *How to Be a Hostage and Live*. Secaucus, NJ: Lyle Stuart, 1987.

Bolz, Captain Frank, and Edward Hershey. *Hostage Cop*. New York: Rawson, Wade Publishers, 1979.

Clutterbuck, Richard. *Kidnap, Hijack and Extortion*. London: Macmillan Press, 1987.

Federal Emergency Management Agency. *Industrial Protection Manual*. 10 vols. Redwood City, CA: Scientific Service, 1981.

Gambordella, Ted. *Fight for Your Life!* Boulder, CO: Paladin Press, 1982.

Goad, K.J.W., and D.H.J. Halsey. *Ammunition [Including Grenades & Mines]*. Oxford, England: Brassey's Publishers, 1982.

Herbert, Anthony B. *Complete Security Handbook*. New York: Collier Books, 1983.

Knowles, Graham. *Bomb Security Guide*. Boston: Butterworth Publishers, 1976.

Livingstone, Neil C. *The War against Terrorism*. 7th printing. Lexington, MA: Lexington Books, 1986.

Livingstone, Neil C., and Terrell E. Arnold. *Fighting Back: Winning the War against Terrorism*. 4th printing. Lexington, MA: Lexington Books, 1987.

Livingstone, Neil C., and Terrell E. Arnold. *Beyond the Iran-Contra Crisis: The Shape of U.S. Anti-Terrorism Policy in the Post-Reagan Era*. Lexington, MA: Lexington Books, 1988.

Nudell, Mayer, and Norman Antokol. *The Handbook for Effective Emergency and Crisis Management*. Lexington, MA: Lexington Books, 1988.

Savage, Peter. *The Safe Travel Book*. Lexington, MA: Lexington Books, 1988.

Schultz, Donald O. *Principles of Physical Security*. Houston: Gulf Publishing, 1978.

Scotti, Anthony. *Executive Safety & International Terrorism*. Englewood Cliffs, NJ: Prentice-Hall, 1986.

Scotti, Anthony. *Police Driving Techniques*. Englewood Cliffs, NJ: Prentice-Hall, 1988.

Smith, C.J. Marchant, and P.R. Haslam. *Small Arms & Cannons*. Oxford, England: Brassey's Publishers, 1982.

Stockholm International Peace Research Institute. *Anti-Personnel Weapons*. London: Taylor & Francis, 1978.

Telecommunication Publishing Inc. *Protecting Your Privacy*.

U.S. Army. *Individual Protective Measures Against Terrorism*. Field circular. U.S. Army Command and General Staff College, Fort Leavenworth, Kansas, 1987.

U.S. Marine Corps. *Terrorism Counteraction*. Quantico, VA: Marine Corps Development and Education Command, 1984.

Index

Research and Advisory Assistance

David Chatellier is senior vice president of Corporate Training Unlimited (CTU). He spent twenty years in the U.S. military, largely in the field of covert and clandestine operations. He specialized in photographic and electronic surveillance, conducting surreptitious entries, doing electronic sweeps, and engaged in the technical collection of intelligence. He carried out numerous operations to ascertain the vulnerability of various military security systems and spent several years instructing Defense Department personnel in such activities. He served in Europe and Vietnam and with the U.S. Rapid Deployment Force.

Donald Feeney, president of CTU, spent fifteen years with the U.S. Army. Upon completion of basic training and AIT, he volunteered for Ranger School and Airborne School at Fort Benning, Georgia. A platoon leader with the 82nd Airborne Division at Fort Bragg, North Carolina, he became proficient at skills such as ambushes, patrolling, raids, reconnaissance, and airborne operations. Mr. Feeney was involved with the reactivation of the 1st Ranger battalion. In this connection, he trained and led a Ranger battalion squad in the conduct of low-visibility raids and special operations in sensitive environments.

In 1978, Mr. Feeney became one of the first members of the U.S. Delta Force, where he spent eight years involved in antiterrorist training and operations. During this period, he was a member of the team sent in 1980 to rescue American hostages in Iran, which ended at Desert One; provided executive protection for senior U.S. diplomats, including the U.S. ambassador in Beirut; and was part of the U.S. operation Urgent Fury in Grenada.

STEVE RYAN, a graduate of Wesleyan University, is a Washington-based writer and researcher. In preparation for a series of articles that he wrote, Mr. Ryan spent two months in Northern Ireland collecting information about the IRA.

CORPORATE TRAINING UNLIMITED is an international security firm founded in 1985. Located in Fayetteville, North Carolina, near Fort Bragg, the special operations hub of the U.S. Army and the home of the elite Delta Force counterterrorist unit, CTU's staff is composed exclusively of former Delta Force and special operations veterans. The company provides counterterrorist, crisis management, executive protection, and physical security services and training to corporations and government agencies.

About the Author

Neil C. Livingstone is an author, lecturer, and frequent media commentator on terrorism and national security issues. He advises major governments and corporations on security matters and crisis management. Formerly a senior executive in an international security company, today Mr. Livingstone serves as an adjunct professor in Georgetown University's National Security Studies program, as consulting editor to the Lexington Books *Issues in Low-Intensity Conflict* series, and as president of the Institute on Terrorism and Subnational Conflict. Mr. Livingstone has served on advisory panels to the secretary of state and the chief of naval operations and has also appeared before the vice president's Task Force for Combatting Terrorism. He is a former consultant to the ABC News show "20/20" and CBS's "The Equalizer."

Mr. Livingstone has written five books on national security topics and more than 60 articles, monographs, and chapters in books. He has delivered some 140 major speeches and appeared on more than 130 television programs, including "Nightline," the "Today" show, "Good Morning America," "Crossfire," the "MacNeil-Lehrer Newshour," and all three evening network news programs.

Mr. Livingstone's 1987 article (with David Halevy) "The Ollie We Knew," which was published in *The Washingtonian* and syndicated by *The New York Times,* was named by the 1988 *Media Guide* as "One of the 10 best stories of the year from the print media."